Why Aren't We Rich Yet?

A 3-Step Plan for Filling Your Plate While Working from Home

Andy Willoughby
with Dr. David Baldwin

WHY AREN'T WE RICH YET? A 3-Step Plan for Filling Your Plate While Working from Home

© 2011 by Promise Enterprises, Inc.

> All rights reserved. No portion of this book may be reproduced or transmitted in any form or by any means—electronic, mechanical, photocopy, recording, scanning, or other—except for brief quotations in critical reviews or articles, without the prior written permission of the publisher.

Published by Christian Life Publications
P.O. Box 8786, Columbus, Georgia

Unless otherwise indicated, Scripture quotations are taken from The New King James Version. ©1982 by Thomas Nelson, Inc.

ISBN: 978-0-9831260-3-4

Contents

Dedication		5
Preface		7
Introduction		13

Part I   Right Thinking

Chapter 1	*Impossible Dream* Syndrome	29
Chapter 2	*Bogeyman* Syndrome	41
Chapter 3	*Cheese and Whine* Syndrome	49
Chapter 4	*Mañana* Syndrome	57
Chapter 5	*Einstein* Syndrome	63
Chapter 6	*Pass the Buck* Syndrome	71

Part II   Winning Habits

Chapter 7	*Superman* Syndrome	81
Chapter 8	*Saddling Up* Syndrome	85
Chapter 9	*Missing Link* Syndrome	91
Chapter 10	*Hobby* Syndrome	101
Chapter 11	*Rescue Mission* Syndrome	107
Chapter 12	*Jack-in-the-Box* Syndrome	113
Chapter 13	*Lone Ranger* Syndrome	121
Chapter 14	*Octopus* Syndrome	129
Chapter 15	*Foreign Missionary* Syndrome	135
Chapter 16	*I've Arrived* Syndrome	141

Conclusion		149
Acknowledgments		151
Notes		153

Dedication

This book is dedicated to my co-author, Dr. David Baldwin. David was killed in a car accident only months before it was printed. David had been my friend for almost forty years. I first met him when he was a young pastor in a small Missouri town. He worked with me in the Christian Radio industry for over a dozen years. I watched him go through hard times and good times, and I never saw his faith or trust in God waver. I am thankful for this book as it put us working together again and renewed our friendship. David's departure was a great loss and a shock due to its unexpectedness. Certainly, it is the loss of those of us still here that loved him, as I never met a man any more prepared to walk into heaven than David. In spite of his many talents and gifts, he was probably the most humble man I will ever know. Well done, Dr. David Baldwin.

~Andy Willoughby

Preface

I had conducted a recruiting session in Long Island, New York. Two weeks later, I returned to train the new distributors, and among them were a lady and her husband. They approached me at the break, and with a caustic, attacking tone the husband said, "What I want to know is—*when are we going to make some money?*"

This training was his first exposure to the business and products. His wife had made the initial purchase and commitment. It appeared that he expected that the purchase of a signup kit and a few products meant windows of heaven should open and money begin pouring down. He failed to understand that they were starting a business. He had not purchased the golden goose for fifty dollars that was overdue for golden eggs.

I have seen this kind of thing happen a lot in this industry. People attend a meeting or get on a conference call and listen to someone talk about how they are making two thousand to twenty thousand dollars a month. They sign up, purchase a few products, and wait for something to happen. They place their kit on the desk or in the corner and occasionally check to see if any *new recruits jump out.* In the beginning, they check it every couple days, then weekly, and eventually monthly. After six months they still do not see any new recruits materializing right before their eyes. So they respond, *"I knew this wouldn't work!"* Then they meticulously store the kit in a place where they never have to look at it again.

Networking is a great business, but it is misunderstood and poorly applied by many. Unrealistic expectations and a "genie in the bottle" mentality run rampant. Sometimes it is because they do not know what to do, and sometimes they just do not want to do what they know to do. Most people start their own network marketing business with the greatest intention of succeeding. But many still end up with an empty plate and frustrated, wondering why they *aren't rich yet.* The goal of this book is to help you know what to do and how to overcome obstacles that threaten your success, then have the drive to do it.

What is the magic of network marketing? The answer: There is *no magic!* It is a business like any other business. You build a clientele and get paid a portion of the sales price. You use a product and refer it to others. You, in essence, get paid on the purchases created by your referrals. What makes it possible for networks to be so financially rewarding is that you also can get paid on the referrals of your referrals and have the ability to leverage your time and efforts with the time and efforts of others.

~ Preface ~

*N*etwork *marketing may be simple, but it is not easy.* It is attainable and, in my opinion, the most efficient way for most people to make money. However, you cannot make an enormous amount of money by simply signing up. To be successful, you need to treat it like a business, not a lottery ticket. Like any other business, it needs to be planned, managed, and diligently worked. I hope that does not sound too serious because this business is a lot of fun. I have enjoyed more travel, relationships, sense of self-worth, and achievement as a result of networking than any other business endeavor. Also, I have made a whole lot of money. I hope that this book will help you get some, if not all, of those things, too!

A network marketing expert wrote that his research showed there are three main reasons that people become involved in network marketing.

1. *A significant cause*— loving the products and believing that they will in some small way improve life *as they know it.* One of humans' greatest fears is to die without having made a difference in their world.

2. *Recognition*— being on a team where they can receive acknowledgement and appreciation for successful efforts. It is a chance to be part of something bigger than they are.

3. *Money and freedom*— understanding that money brings opportunities. Lots of money adds up to plenty of choices; little money equals few choices. The more money they acquire, the more options they will have.[1]

Frankly, I think, for the most part, those three are the reasons people stay in networking. I believe that most people get into networking because they want freedom. Everybody wants freedom. It is either for freedom of time, money or choices. Let's start with time. The leveraging ability of networking can give you the capacity to earn more income in less time. You enjoy compensation from the combined efforts of your networking team, allowing you to earn more. I will talk more about this concept later in the book. How about choices? To me, being able to make your own choices is one, if not the most important, benefit of networking. I decide when I work, where I work, and when and where I play. I have always been the type of guy who would rather be captain of a rowboat than first mate of a battleship, so that works for me. Now, let's talk about money. Network marketing is one of the few ways that the average person can obtain wealth. I mean real wealth, like getting rich. Everybody wants to be rich. Even people who say they do not want to be rich want to be rich. Getting rich is rational. Living poor is irrational. Living with just enough seems sensible, but having more than enough means you can share and save. I cannot verify any accounts of anyone who became wealthy by a lottery or any other unforeseen method that simply turned down the wealth. I also have no knowledge of anyone who earned wealth and then gave it all away while they still had a considerable life expectancy. I am just saying that it is normal and human to want wealth. It does not mean you are backslidden, vain, or carnal to desire a prosperous life. True riches come with the wisdom to control wealth, rather than to let it control you. My hope is that if you use some of the principles from this book to obtain wealth, you will as diligently seek the wisdom to manage it at the same time.

So let's get on about the business of succeeding in networking. There are predictable reasons why networking businesses succeed or fail. In the following sixteen chapters, you will discover common characteristics, or *syndromes*, of unhealthy businesses. A *syndrome* is a set of symptoms characteristic of a specific disorder or disease.[2] In other words, syndromes speak of patterns of failure, breakdown, collapse, and potential disappointment in your business. For each syndrome you will be given a clear-cut, 3-step plan to ensure a strong, vigorous, and healthy business.

Why Aren't We Rich Yet? is written for both new distributors and network marketing professionals, but I do not think you will have to be a network marketer to gain from it. I believe you will find that the principles will transfer into other industries as well.

~ Preface ~

I hope it will balance beliefs with behavior, vision with venture, and right attitudes with right actions.

The first six chapters deal with the *mind game* and the importance of having the right mindset. The second part addresses *cultivating winning habits* and advantages of developing effective daily disciplines. The aim of this book is to equip you with both right *attitudes* and right *actions*.

Introduction

Why Network Marketing?

*R*ecent estimates place network marketing as a $200 billion a year industry with more than forty-five million distributors worldwide. Studies reveal there are fifteen million distributors in the United States alone.[1]

Why should you consider starting your own home-based network marketing business?

- The average home-based business household earns nearly twice as much as the average American household.

- In recent years, network marketing has been increasing at twice the growth rate of the economy.

- Networking is the least expensive way to start a home business.

- Network marketing offers the least risk as you do not have to quit your job or borrow a lot of money to get started.

- Home-based business owners accumulate more tax deductions than any other labor group in America.

- Network marketing yields *more money* for *less work* in *less time* than any other kind of business.

Did you know that the gap between the rich and the poor is the largest since record keeping began? If you consider yourself to be in the middle class, you may be losing ground. It is only prudent to start thinking about alternative ways to earn an income.

Unconventional income options, such as network marketing, will continue to expand due to the lack of job security in the United States and low-cost labor competition from foreign countries. Today we are competing for manufacturing jobs with a billion people in China who are working for as little as twenty-five to fifty cents an hour. Computer and software technicians from India and the Philippines are working for one-third to one-half what is earned in the United States. I saw a magazine article talking about a major airline manufacturer hiring three hundred Russian engineers because they would work for one-half of what their American counterparts would earn.[2] Manufacturing may go to cheap labor in other countries. Fortunately, network marketing is not involved with manufacturing, but rather *distribution.*

Several times in the last fifteen years, Bill Gates, founder of Microsoft, has been rated the richest man in the world. Do you know why? It is because Sam Walton, the founder of Wal-Mart, died and split his fortune up among his heirs. If Sam were still alive, he would probably still hold that title as he did for multiple years before his death. Wal-Mart is not a manufacturer, but it is a very successful distributor. Sam Walton became the richest man in the world because of distribution. Network marketing gives the average person access to the distribution sector of the economy without the large financial risk of traditional business. To compete in a global market, it takes a great deal of expertise and money. Network marketing bridges the gap by combining the products of big business with the distributing efforts of entrepreneurs.

The economy has changed forever. I believe we are in a time when the family farm will return. I do not really mean *farm* because the large corporate farms have already taken over that sector of the economy. I am talking about a return to entrepreneurism. A huge percentage of the millions in America who have lost their jobs, been downsized, or had their pay cut will never find jobs again that will afford them the lifestyle they have been used to experiencing. Those who are not willing to

~ Introduction ~

accept that sentence are going to have to get into business for themselves.

Within every big movement in America, it has always been those that distributed the products that made the fortunes. In Gold Rush days it was the trading posts, not the miners, who made the most money. Now that we are in a global market, we find products on store shelves from all over the world. The companies and employees who make those products are earning from the purchases of people in other countries. It is easy to find a reliable network marketing company that will give you the opportunity to earn in other countries. You might think, "I don't know people in other countries." Well, I did not either, but today I earn from the efforts of other entrepreneurs in dozens of countries because I knew someone who knew someone who knew someone in another country.

What Is Network Marketing...*Really*?

Wikipedia, an on-line encyclopedia, defines *network marketing* or *multi-level marketing* as "a business model that combines direct marketing with franchising." Network marketing functions by recruiting distributors, independent business owners, to sell a product and offer additional commissions based on the sales of people recruited into their network or, as it is commonly called, down-line. This arrangement is similar to

~ Introduction ~

franchise arrangements where royalties are paid from the sales of individual franchise operations to the franchisor as well as to an area or regional manager.

Network marketing is legal in over one hundred countries, including the United States. Millions of people are engaged in networking businesses worldwide. It is certainly not a new concept and is an evolving industry continuing to gain momentum.

There are many companies that market their products in this manner, including XanGo, Quixstar or Amway, Avon, Mary Kay, Herbal Life, Noni, NuSkin, and Shaklee (I am sorry if I missed your company, there are just too many good companies to name them all). The independent distributor is the marketing arm of this distribution enterprise. It is the distributor's job to move product, usually done by word of mouth, which is called *referral marketing.*

Network marketing does not care if you have a college degree, if you are young or old, tall or thin, what the color of your skin is, or if you are male or female. It does not care if you are new to the industry or a seasoned veteran. Network marketing only cares about what you will do *now*.

The core principle that drives network marketing is people using products and referring it to other people that use the products that refer to other people and so on. In the beginning, network marketing companies like Avon focused on the retail side of the business. Today, the trend is to focus less on retail with more emphasis being placed on the franchise concept.

One of the chief advantages of starting a network marketing business is that nearly anyone can afford to get started. Let's contrast that with starting a conventional business:

- Conventional businesses are risky to start, and most fail within five years.

- Franchises are safer but very expensive, and you rarely have any freedom until you have expanded to having many locations. In the meantime, you have worked your life away, many times putting in so many hours that your actual per hour earnings are less than what you could make at a job. I have a friend who purchased a burger restaurant franchise and eventually owned three. He and his wife were working eighty hours a week trying to make it work. He spent a million dollars starting each restaurant. In contrast, my networking franchise cost me $35 to start and the overhead was product I used anyway. After a few years my monthly volume was over 3.5 million dollars a month. Do the numbers tell you which one is the best deal?

- A home-based networking business usually only costs a few hundred dollars to start and offers enough tax benefits to pay for the products you buy for your own personal use. That makes this whole concept a no-brainer.

I have a friend who borrowed money against his house to start his own business. It was a business in an industry in which he was very familiar. Unfortunately, the business did not work out; he went bankrupt and lost $100,000. He did not just lose equity in his house. He lost his house.

What drives people to take these kinds of risks? A recent national survey by Hewlett Packard Company revealed that eighty percent of business owners said they had a business because they wanted to be their own boss, seventy percent said they wanted to earn their own income, and ninety percent said they liked the freedom to make their own decisions.[3]

That same friend who lost his house in a failed business attempt spent a few months building a network marketing business. In those few months he actually worked, he found one person who was serious about building a business. My friend collected a nice added income for many years, enjoying the residual income from that one referral. It is a shame he did not take the business seriously and find a few more partners to earn enough to make up for his losses from the traditional business endeavor.

At the time of this writing, Emma Lyman is seventy-nine years old. She has no higher education and her only work experience is working eight months as a telephone receptionist.

~ Introduction ~

Yet, over the past twenty years she has consistently been among the top two percent of income earners in America. She did it without any big risk, and in the beginning she did it while working her receptionist job.

Everyone knows someone who has tried network marketing and failed, but everyone also knows someone who has tried a traditional business and failed. The difference is that those who start a networking business rarely lose their house or savings. Why? It costs very little to get started. Most people starting a traditional business usually have to give up their jobs to start the business. However, network marketing can be done part-time while working full-time elsewhere.

If you have a son-in-law that successfully supports your daughter and grandchildren and has the drive to be an entrepreneur, would you rather he give up his job and mortgage their house to start his own business or start working from home part-time? I think the answer is obvious. Many times when a family member gets involved in network marketing, rather than receiving encouragement and support, they are scolded or humiliated. Critics of network marketing often ignore the low start-up cost and minimal risk factor of this type of business. Don't you think that network marketing demands a second look?

Simply put, entrepreneurs desire to improve their lives and take control of their futures. Those that choose network marketing face very little risk with the potential of tremendous reward. It is not a get-rich-quick scheme. It is a legal, ethical, and very practical way for a person to earn extra money or replace a job. Many of the top achievers in this industry have gone on to earn a literal fortune.

Let's review some of the benefits of building a network marketing business.

1. Low risk: You can normally start a business for less than $500.00. If it is over that, you should be careful. There is very little overhead. You probably already have most of the tools you will need. You will not need to pay for office space and extra utilities. If someone tells you to rent an office for your network marketing business, you better run. Also, you do not have to risk your current job. Most successful networkers initially started part time. They only left their jobs after more than replacing their incomes with networking.

2. Freedom with time: You will manage your own schedule, but you will have to have a schedule. You can work around family and church commitments. If you work weekends and holidays, it is because you will choose to do so. Once you have built your business, you can maintain it with much fewer hours. You will be able to take vacations when you desire and for pretty much as long as you choose. Because I have built a network marketing business, I go to bed when I get tired and get

up when I wake up. I can take my wife out for dinner in the middle of the week, and my grandson out fishing at nine o'clock on Tuesday morning.

3. Unlimited earning potential: I know networkers who make a few hundred dollars a month and I know those that make several hundred thousand dollars a month. Your income is decided by your ambition and drive. At the writing of this book, I make over five times as much money at networking than I earned as vice-president of a group of radio stations, and I work less than half the hours.

4. Tax savings: If you are working part-time at your business and have a full-time job, there are usually enough legal tax benefits for the networker to pay for the products you buy for your own personal use. I know of one lady who before networking was getting a tax refund of between $1,000 and $1,500 a year. A few years later, she lost a deduction and still got over $8,000 back.

5. Travel: If you like to travel, most companies offer many reward trips for their hardest working distributors. I have been all over the world on trips paid for by the companies I was working with. Also, there are many legal tax deductions for travel.

6. **Leverage:** You can build a big business and still have a life because of leverage. It takes a big network to make big money, but you do not have to do it all yourself. If you just find three people who find three people who find three people, by the time you get to the ninth level, or generation, you would have over two thousand in your network! In my personal network I have over 100,000 distributors, and 99% of those come from just four main leaders in my business.

7. **Security:** This business is your own; you get paid for your efforts. It does not matter how old you are or who likes or dislikes you. If the economy slows down and you need more money, you just work harder. When times get tough in networking, you do not get laid off. The companies just start offering more incentives for you to work harder.

Why Aren't We Rich Yet?

Part I

Right Thinking

*H*ave you noticed that a cat always lands on its feet? Realizing it is falling, a cat gets its head in the right position, and its feet automatically follow. A big part of succeeding is getting personal thoughts and attitudes in the right position. When you get your head straight, the right behaviors will naturally tag along. The first few chapters deal with getting your thinking straight.

Chapter 1

Impossible Dream
Syndrome

*A*re you a victim of the *Impossible Dream* Syndrome? The concept of starting your own business and being financially independent is appealing. You could have no financial worries and earn the respect of your peers, but you feel like Don Quixote. It just sounds too good to be true; it is the *Impossible Dream*. Perhaps for you, it *is* impossible! Why? In your heart-of-hearts you do not believe it *will ever happen*. It is beyond your ability to envision anything *that* life-altering ever happening to you. It is difficult to wrap your imagination around such an overwhelming vision. The key issue of the *Impossible Dream* Syndrome is *belief.*

The underlying problem is that you lack confidence to succeed in *this* business or, for that matter, *any* business. Simply put, the problem is not your supplier, products, up-line or down-line. It is—*you!* Author Woodrow Kroll stated, "Our greatest enemy is often ourselves."[1] In this case, you may be your own worst enemy. You believe that it is truly the *Impossible Dream* and it will forever remain out of reach!

Everyone tends to act in a manner consistent with his or her self-concept. Solomon said, "What a man thinks, so is he" (Proverbs 23:7). Henry Ford put it this way: "If you think you can do a thing or think you can't do a thing, you're right."[2] Dr. Richard D. Dobbins wrote, "Your self-concept colors everything you see in life. It is the lens through which you look at life."[3] Brian Tracy chimed in, "Whatever you truly believe with feeling becomes reality."[4] What you believe may not even be *right*, but to you it is *real*, and you will react accordingly.

John Hammond in his book, *The Fine Art of Doing Better*, shares about the Great Houdini. In the early 1900's, Henry Houdini traveled throughout the United States touting that there was not a county jail that could hold him for more than fifteen minutes. Ordinarily, within a few minutes he was strutting down the street, with the townsfolk applauding enthusiastically. However, there was that *one time*. Five minutes turned into fifteen minutes that soon became one hour. He was listening for a slight *click* indicating the lock had been picked, allowing the jail door to open. He *never heard it!* After two-and-a-half hours, he collapsed exhausted against the door, only to discover the door opening wide. *It had never been locked!* It was locked only

~ *Impossible Dream* Syndrome ~

in his mind, and to him it *was* reality. *Even the Great Houdini could not unlock an unlocked door.*[5]

People with the *Impossible Dream* Syndrome are usually great spectators. They show up at events and celebrate the success of others, but they do not get in the game themselves. They think the opportunity is great. They tell everyone exactly what they are going to do. They write goals, share with friends, and convince everyone (but themselves) of great things they will accomplish. But, deep down they just do not believe it is going to work for them, and it *doesn't!*

Some people say, "I'm going to *try* network marketing and see if it works." You do not try network marketing; you do network marketing. Trying to do something is leaving your self-esteem an escape route should you not put in the effort to actually succeed. A contrasting mentality would be that of the commander that once landed on the enemies' shore and ordered his men to burn their own ships. The soldiers quickly realized that their only choice was to conquer the territory or die trying. There was absolutely no opportunity for retreating.

For many years we had a swimming pool in our backyard. This pool was a great source of fun and entertainment for our whole family. There were many barbecues and swim parties. I have a lot of great memories from our family time around that pool. An observation I made from watching people get into the pool taught me a good lesson about succeeding. People get into a swimming pool in one of two ways. They either jump in all at once and deal with the shock quickly, or they get into the water in increments, inches at a time, slowly and painfully. One thing I did notice was that all of those that just jumped in went swimming. However, a good percentage of those that got in slowly turned around and went back. They were dressed for the occasion and got their feet wet, but surrendered to the conditions before they reached their goal. To succeed you will eventually have to decide to just dive in and quit testing the water. That is just the way it is in life.

3-STEP PLAN FOR BUILDING BELIEF AND CONVICTION

FIRST STEP: Recognize your personal belief system.

It is time to take inventory (no, not of your products) of yourself. Changing your belief system is the starting point. The following pattern is a belief system:

~Your **beliefs** drive your **thoughts** that drive your **emotions** that drive your **actions** that determine **results** and decide your **destiny**.~

Belief systems work both positively and negatively. What you accept in your heart about yourself will shape your *life blueprints.* Be very careful to guard your heart. Fear of failure, rejection, or punishment can potentially contaminate a healthy belief system.

Remember, your *beliefs* influence your thought life. The way you *think* decides how you *feel*, and how you *feel* establishes how you *act.* Your actions *form habits* that ultimately *determine your destiny.*

It is equally true that if you are currently succeeding, yet in your heart-of-hearts you see yourself as an ultimate loser, it is only a matter of time before you will sabotage your success. You will eventually act out what is in your heart!

Fortunately, you can reprogram your beliefs to align with your best possible future. Whether you know it or not, you are constantly talking to yourself. You might want to listen to these inward conversations.

Here is a helpful exercise to help you examine your self-talk. Get a piece of paper and number down the left-hand side from one to twenty. At the top of the page, write, "*I AM.*" Write twenty statements beginning with *I AM*. Do not deliberate long; just write the first thing that pops into your mind. Maybe your first statement could be: "I am wondering what to write next." Now, you only have nineteen more to go. Remember, there is no right or wrong answer.

If you have more negative I AM's than positive ones, you may be moving forward with an inward brake depressed.

Perhaps, you are constantly criticizing yourself and not even aware of it.

It is difficult to live with a critical person, especially when that person is you! You can escape from others, but you cannot get away from yourself.

Identify and challenge any pseudo-beliefs you have about yourself. Consider if any of the following examples apply to you:

1.) Those in your *center of influence* tell you how talented you are and you just *cannot see it.*

2.) Those around you see you succeeding, but you only see yourself failing.

3.) People pay you compliments and you have a difficult time receiving them and tend to diminish their kind words in some way.

Some people have a deep-seated belief that they do not deserve to succeed. They feel guilty about something they have done in the past. Some actually believe that they do not deserve to succeed because of something someone in their family has done. Nothing disqualifies you from deserving success. It may complicate the process, but it does not make it wrong for you to succeed. I remember as a child walking down a stairway in our home, holding a belt in my hand and snapping it like a whip. (I do not know why little boys can pretty well turn about anything they pick up into some kind of weapon.) As I passed by the glass door to the front of our house, the buckle hit a glass pane and broke it. No one saw or heard my dastardly deed but me, which meant "not me" did it. After all, there were five other kids in the house that could have done it. I did not need an alibi—just anonymity. I was never caught for that transgression, but I remember going upstairs and using that belt to try and spank myself. Now, if I had confessed my sin, it is highly unlikely that my parents would have spanked me. It was, after all, an accident. So in truth I was harder on myself than others would have been. My shortcomings were much larger in my eyes than in the eyes of those around me. I hope you are not still trying to spank yourself for something that happened long ago.

People fail because of their circumstances. Achievers succeed *in spite* of circumstances. Self-pity will always justify failure. You cannot afford to give yourself an excuse to fail. Accept the fact that, no matter the circumstances, you *will* achieve your dreams!

STEP 2: Build basics into your business.

Former NFL coach of the Green Bay Packers, Vince Lombardi, began training camp each year with his legendary words, *"Gentlemen, this is a football."* He then reminded these seasoned football players of the most basic objectives of the game. Why? He understood that his team would succeed only to the degree that they executed the basics of the game. It is alleged that after a particularly crushing defeat, Lombardi addressed the men on the bus with, "*Gentlemen, this is a football!* The object of the game is to move this ball from one end of the field to the other end." A voice from the back of the bus was heard saying, "Coach, you're going too fast. Can you repeat that?"[6]

Build your business with the ***foundation*** of ***belief*** and ***conviction***. Then, add a level of ***prospecting***. Next, add a level of honest, concise, and ***persuasive presenting***. Lastly, add a pointed ***close***.

Conviction means "having a fixed or firm belief."[7] There are a number of things you can do to *fix or firm-up belief* in your success.

- *Read books.* When you read, it makes everything you do more "do-able!" Plus, it provides a seedbed for new ideas.

- *Listen to tapes, CDs, podcasts, holograms or whatever the electronic information delivery system is when you read this statement.* You have access to a "university" of wisdom in your car. Simply turn off the radio and listen to informative, motivational recordings whenever possible.

- *Go to events, meetings, and conferences.* Leaders are born at events! At an event, someone will tell his or her story, and you will have an "ah-ha" moment. You suddenly realize, *"If that ordinary person can do it, I can surely do it, too!"* These meetings are books with skin on them. You see and hear real people share how they did or are doing what you want to do. It will put the tangibility into the business for you. All of the great leaders attend the events. I have heard many people say, "I don't need that to motivate me." I have never met a person who had already achieved top ranks in his or her company say that. They are at the meetings and events, not only for themselves, but also to help others. These events have life, and they breathe in and out molecules of success. You are there to receive and give. It is the balance of life. Your attendance will encourage others that are there. Your absence will discourage someone in your circle of influence. So do yourself and others a favor—attend the events.

- *Read and study about the lives of successful people. Whenever possible, get around them.* Success is contagious. Be around people that you want to be like. If you spend your time asking questions and not just trying to show people how smart you are, you will most likely learn something. The lifestyles and habits of successful people are just as contagious as those of losers. Give success a chance—hang around it.

STEP 3: Understand the law of sowing and reaping.

Farmers recognize sowing and reaping as a *natural law*. If farmers did not *believe* in this law, we would all starve to death! A farmer understands that if he sows, cultivates, and fertilizes the soil, *he will get a crop*! He may not know how big of a crop…but he knows that he will, in all likelihood, have *a harvest for his efforts*. Even during dry seasons, he will still get more than he planted.

You will never see a farmer plow his field, sow the seed, fertilize the land, and after a couple of weeks shake his head and say, "Well, I don't see anything coming up. I knew this was a waste of my time and money." There has to be as much *belief* in your network marketing business as a farmer has in his fields.

If you were starting a more traditional business, would you work it with the conviction that you would succeed? You would be crazy to mortgage your house, invest all of your savings, or borrow from your friends or family to start a business if you did not have full conviction that you could succeed. You need to have that degree of belief in your new networking business. Just because it did not cost you much to start the business and you do not have big overhead is no reason to treat the business with less respect than other businesses. The potential for earnings is just as great, and probably greater, than most traditional businesses you could start. So treat it with the respect it deserves.

I have a friend that owned a construction company. When times were lean, he started a network marketing business. His wife joined him to help, even though she worked full-time as a secretary at another job. They both worked hard on their new enterprise. Then the economy in his area turned around, and he immediately stopped sowing into their network marketing company and returned to rev up his construction business. His wife, though, did not miss a beat and continued working the networking business. So, which one really believed in their network marketing company? Do you really believe in your networking business? Do you believe that if you diligently work this business, you will acquire wealth as the harvest for your labor? Then accept it and act like it.

The law of sowing and reaping is both a natural law and a spiritual one. The Apostle Paul recognized it as a *spiritual law* in Galatians 6:7, 9: "whatever a man sows, that he will also reap....And let us not grow weary while doing good, for in due season we shall reap if we do not lose heart."

BOTTOM LINE:
You can succeed if others do not believe in you, but seldom will you succeed if you do not believe in yourself!

Chapter 2

Bogeyman Syndrome

Do you have the *Bogeyman* Syndrome? You desire to excel in your new business and are full of hope and enthusiasm. You see the potential and want it for yourself. You have started your business, but in your heart you know that you are *not* generating enough contacts to justify your hoped-for success. You make excuses that sound reasonable. The key issue of the *Bogeyman* Syndrome is *fear*.

Fear is normal. Ann Landers received ten thousand letters each month and the most predominant problem people wrote about was fear.[1] There are only two groups of people who are completely free from fear: the dead and the deranged. So, if you are alive and not crazy, you will experience fear. Some fears are healthy. You might fear strolling down the center of the highway because you say to yourself, "*I could get killed doing that!*" Some fears are rational and meant to protect. Other fears are silly or disruptive and designed to rob you of your dreams. Deal with your fears when they are small or they will grow up and try to eat you for lunch!

If something is new or appears risky, it is prudent to advance with caution. The skills and activities of building a networking business are new to many people. They have never done it before, so it appears scary. It is like going into a dark room that you have never entered. You do not know what to expect. You are anxious and cautious with your heart pounding out of your chest. So, what do you do? You will either try to find the light switch and turn on the light or try to find someone to lead you through the room.

Facing new challenges necessitates the same two strategies:

1.) *Turning the light on* suggests learning all you can about the business and developing a plan of action. In other words, knowledge is light.

2.) *Finding someone to lead you* speaks of recruiting a mentor. Select someone with a proven and successful history to guide you through the uncertainties of this new endeavor.

~In terms of starting a networking business, you might employ both strategies.~

~ *Bogeyman* Syndrome ~

Fear is a major problem for many people in this business. Some stumble over in-person contacts, while others fret about over-the-phone presentations. When you fear doing any business-building activity, normally, it is because you have either done it infrequently or you have done it before and had a bad (unsuccessful) experience.

3-STEP PLAN FOR OVERCOMING FEAR

FIRST STEP: Keep doing the thing that you fear.

~Ralph Waldo Emerson said, "Do the thing you fear and the death of fear is certain."[2]~

It is true that if you do what you fear, at some point, you will become desensitized to it. Eventually, you will *burn out your fears!*

When I first began traveling for business, I had an *irrational* fear of flying. When I got on an airplane, I knew the plane was going to *crash and burn.* I actually felt sorry for my seatmates and everyone on board. Because they were on an airplane with me, it was going to crash and they had no idea what was coming. There were times when I went to the airport, arrived at the gate, and turned around and went home. (Try to explain that to the boss.) However, the next day I returned to the airport and tried again. It was always easier the next day. The more often I flew, the easier it got. Also, the longer the time was between flights, the harder it became.

Fortunately, I am very comfortable and relaxed flying today. Given half a chance, I sleep on airplanes. How did I overcome the fear of flying? I kept going to the gate. If I went home one day, I went back the next day and got on the plane. Many times, I was terrified the whole trip, but I kept facing my fear. Little by little, the fear diminished. Eventually, it was gone completely.

If your knees buckle, you break out in a sweat, and your heart races before picking up the phone, simply adopt a *just do it* mentality! There is no option; you must face your fears. Keep making the calls, do the follow-up work, and ask for a decision. I promise you that, in time, it will get easier, and you will succeed in networking. You should consistently create enough activity to become comfortable with your efforts. If you find it starts getting harder to do again, it is probably because you let too much time stack up between "flights."

SECOND STEP: See yourself succeeding.

Walt Disney passed away right before the opening of Disney World in Orlando, Florida. Someone approached Disney's long-time creative director, Mike Vance, and commented that it was a

~ *Bogeyman* Syndrome ~

shame that Walt Disney did not see Disney World. Mr. Vance immediately responded, "He did see it—that's why it's here."[3]

What do you see? Do you see yourself succeeding? A creative imagination is invaluable to your success.

You have probably heard the expression, "Well, *seeing is believing!*" In networking you are never going to see it until you believe it! When someone does not see himself or herself succeeding at certain levels, it always becomes an issue.

A friend of mine shared that after teaching on the creative use of imagination, a lady approached him. She said, "Sorry, but I can't relate to your teaching because I have absolutely **no** imagination." His instant retort was, "Wow! That's really great!" She thought that he had misunderstood her so she repeated it again slowly, "I… have…**no**…imagination." He replied, "That's wonderful that you have **no** imagination because *it means you never worry!*" Shocked, she reacted, "Well, *I worry all the time.*" He counseled, "Lady, you *have* an imagination. It's just going in the *wrong direction!*"

Some people worry in "3-D Technicolor with wrap-around sound." They cast their deepest fears on the big screen of their minds and crowd out every optimistic thought. Jesus said not to worry (see Matthew 6:25-34). Do not waste your precious imagination on visualizing failure. It is apparently not good for you. Job said, "For the thing I greatly feared has come upon me, and what I dreaded has happened to me" (Job 3:25). However,

Psalm 112 declares that one "who fears the Lord....will not be afraid of evil tidings; His heart is steadfast, trusting in the Lord." Paul said that "we know that all things work together for good to those who love God, to those who are the called according to His purpose" (Romans 8:28). Learn to assume that all things will work out for the best. Use your imagination to see success in your life.

The imagination is a handy tool. It can produce worry, or it can be channeled in a positive direction. If you can see *the bad* that can happen, you also can see *the potential good.* Instead of your imagination being used to cultivate fear and worry, it can become a source for faith. Hebrews 11:1 states, "Now faith is the substance of things *hoped for,* the evidence of things *not seen"* (italics mine). Do you have the faith to see yourself succeeding in this business?

THIRD STEP: Find a suitable mentor.

It is said that experience is a great teacher, but the tuition is very high? If you are capable of learning from others' experience, you will save yourself a lot of headaches and heartaches. In addition, you will reach your goals sooner.

~There are two ways you will learn in life: *mistakes* and *mentors.*~

~ *Bogeyman* Syndrome ~

I have had many people ask me to be their mentor. In my experience, most individuals did not want a mentor. They wanted me to give them a pill that would instantly give them the success that I have. Usually, the call to request mentorship was the last time I heard from them.

If you want a mentor, *take responsibility for your own learning*. Request to meet regularly with a mentor and *be there*. You cannot expect your mentor to call you every week to see about meeting. In school, it was your responsibility to show up for class; the teacher did not come and get you. *Same here!*

If you are currently being mentored, be sure to *follow directions*. New networkers seem to take great pride in rewriting the text books. I have given new distributors a plan, script or system, and instead of using it they immediately *rewrote it*. They were very proud of the improvements they had made and then wondered why it *did not work*. Do what your mentors ask you to do, or they will quickly tire of you.

You will need diverse mentors to take you to different levels. Find a mentor at each level and work your way up. Attend all of the training sessions of the top leaders, but do not go to the top distributor the first day and say, "I want you to be my personal mentor and teach me everything you know." You must first master lower levels before you can justify a higher level mentor. In networking it is very easy to find a mentor who will benefit by your success. You just go up-line. This is a real advantage over most industries.

Never ask a cross-line leader to be your mentor unless one volunteers. Cross-line leaders do not earn off your work, and it is not fair to ask. If you have trouble finding a mentor, simply research success in your company and industry. Read the books and magazines, and listen to and watch recordings of the successful. These are mentoring tools that anyone can access. It is your business. Do not let "I can't find a mentor" be a crutch for failure. Let the tools and training materials mentor you.

BOTTOM LINE:

"God has not given us a spirit of fear, but of power and of love and of a sound mind" (2 Timothy 1:7). God admonishes us 365 times in Scripture to "Fear not!" It is God's daily promise to you!

Chapter 3

Cheese and Whine
Syndrome

Do you have the *Cheese and Whine* Syndrome? If so, others may often hear you say, "It's just *too* hard!" "*Why* did I start this business?" "I wish it was *easier*!" "I thought I would be *rich* by now." "I don't think I'll *make* it!" The key issue of the *Cheese and Whine* Syndrome is *rejection*.

My initial response to each of these statements is, "Do you want cheese with that *whine*?" Millions of people get involved with networking because they want the cheese (benefits). It offers a higher quality lifestyle, freedom, great money, quality relationships, security, residual income, and use of premium products. But then they *whine* about how hard it is to get. Let me give you a practical perspective.

~Networking is simple, but it is not easy!~

Nothing that pays this well is going to be easy. Obviously, it is not hard work physically. You might carry a box or two occasionally, but it is certainly *not* manual labor. It is not even hard mentally. Basically, what you do is use a product you like and refer it to others. Not exactly brain surgery, *is it?* Most people do that all the time for free. They eagerly and enthusiastically recommend products, movies, restaurants, doctors, dentists, and so on. If it is something you are already doing, why is it *not easy*? The reason is that you must overcome one of life's greatest emotional challenges—*rejection.*

Rejection is the reason networking pays so well. The harder it is to get a *yes*, the more they will pay you because of a *no*. Do not forget that *no's* are your friend. As long as people are saying *"no,"* your company will pay you to find those that will say *"yes."* Without rejection your company would not need you. They would simply send out a letter, and people would join the company and keep using the product.

A clerk at Wal-Mart will get a *yes* easily and not many *no's*, but the job does not pay nearly as well as network marketing. Learn to deal with rejection! Rejection is the reason that your business opportunity will never become over-saturated.

3-STEP PLAN FOR OVERCOMING REJECTION

STEP 1: Expect, appreciate, and embrace rejection!

Do not let rejection become personal. They are *not* rejecting you; they are rejecting the opportunity. Give people the freedom to make up their minds. If they choose not to join or buy, respect it!

A father and his little girl were on an elevator when a beautiful young lady joined them. After going up a few floors, the young lady turned around and abruptly slapped the father, then exited quickly from the elevator. He was dumfounded, thinking, *"What did I do to her?"* As the elevator continued, the little girl said to her father, "That woman was mean, wasn't she, Daddy?" The father nodded and said, "She hit me hard." "I know," the little girl said, "and when she got on the elevator, she stepped on my toe. So I pinched her."

Likewise, do not take a *no* personally. Most of the time, it has nothing to do with you. It is just where that person is in life at the moment. There are lots of people in this world. If you put your offer in front of enough people, you will find those that will join you.

Reasons people give for rejecting your proposal are seldom the *real* reasons. In fact, you may never know the real reasons. Even the Bible says that buyers are liars! "'It is good for nothing,' cries the buyer; but when he has gone his way, then he boasts" (Proverbs 20:14).

Nobody can please everybody all of the time. As good as your company may be, it is not for everyone. Some may love the product and business opportunity, but the timing is off. With others the timing may be right, but, for whatever reason, they do not see the product or business concept as a match.

If your family and friends are rejecting you, the best way to prove them wrong is by moving on and building your business without them. Understand that your family and friends are waiting on you. When they say *no* to your opportunity, they are really saying, "Let's see how *you* do first. Maybe I will consider it if you do *well.*"

I can guarantee you that once your friends and relatives have told you *no*, you will **never** get them to join until you have proven that you can do it without them. That does not mean you have to be making a million dollars a year to impress them. They just need to see progress and a continued positive effort.

SECOND STEP: Do something positive every day.

~The path to success is taking one good step after another in the right direction on a daily basis.~

~ *Cheese and Whine* Syndrome ~

Discover that your real competition is not with others; it is with yourself. The secret of your future is hidden in your daily routines. You will never change your life until you change something you do on a daily basis.

Whatever you practice, you will become. Practice being rude, and you will become a rude person. Practice speaking critically of others, and you will become a critical person. If you argue a lot, you will become an argumentative person. Practice doing at least one successful thing every day, and you will become a successful person.

You do not have to be great to start, but you have to start to be great. *Some people cannot stand to be small long enough to become big.* Zechariah 4:10 says, "Do not despise these small **beginnings**, for the Lord rejoices to see the work begin" (New Living Translation, my emphasis).

You must start doing the little things continually and often enough to create enough momentum to become successful. Building a networking organization is like most things you build in life. You start with the foundation, which takes a large percentage of the actual construction time, and most of it is out of sight. A successful person has simply formed the habits of doing things on a regular basis with very little recognition or payback in the beginning that unsuccessful people will not do.

A habit is formed by doing the same thing every day for at least twenty-one days. Promise yourself that for the next twenty-one days you will discipline yourself to form a new habit concerning your networking business. Then keep track of your efforts.

You decide your habits, and your habits decide your future. You will never change your life until you change something you do every day. Our lives are a reflection of our habits.

THIRD STEP: Know that perseverance pays well!

The word *persevere* comes from the Latin words *per* and *severus* which mean "through" and "severe," respectively. It implies that perseverance is *pressing through severe circumstances.*

Rejection is tough to handle. Former President Harry Truman used to say, *"If you can't stand the heat, get out of the kitchen."*[1] In other words, if you want the time, money and freedom that the *networking life* offers, you must put up with some discomfort and uneasiness. The important thing to remember is that *it will be worth it!*

It is not as important that you start well as it is that you finish well. If you persist long enough, you will inherit the efforts of those that quit too soon.

~"The end of a thing is better than its beginning; The patient in spirit is better than the proud in spirit" (Ecclesiastes 7:8).~

One-hit wonders are those artists that had a single great hit and then were never heard from again. But legends are those that continued to have multiple hits over long and distinguished careers. In fact, many legendary artists spent many years working, singing, writing, and traveling prior to their first hits. That speaks well of their persistent personalities. It is said that *over-night success* only takes fifteen years.

BOTTOM LINE:

Helen Keller said, "We can do anything we want as long as we stick to it long enough." What counts is not who is first to start, but, rather, who is the last one to quit! Remember that a "big shot" is just a "little shot" that just kept shooting. So stay tough and stick with it!

Chapter 4

Mañana
Syndrome

Do you have the *Mañana* Syndrome? *Mañana* is a Spanish word meaning *tomorrow*. Do you often put things off until tomorrow? Do you rationalize that it will be easier the next day, but you never quite get around to the task? The key issue of the *Mañana* Syndrome is *procrastination*.

Procrastinate means "to defer action; delay; to put off until another day or time."[1] People tend to procrastinate concerning things they either do not like or are afraid to do.

It is possible that from early childhood you were never made to do anything you did not want to do. As I write this text, I am on an airplane. The young lady in the seat in front of me is being literally terrorized by her small son named Ryan. I know his name because during the first half-hour of the flight, she has said it about a thousand times. He does not want to sit down, hold still, or behave in any way. He is raising a holy war to do only what he wants to do. Strapped in an airplane seat for two-and-a-half hours is the last place a parent wants to teach a child to do something that he or she does not want to do, but sometimes, it is necessary. This young mother would have been much better off to have done the instruction at home and given Ryan his way on the airplane. Ryan is rebelling. Is your procrastination the result of a lifetime of rebellion? You just do not want to do what you do not want to do? If you were rich enough to do only what you wanted to do when you wanted to do it, you probably would not be reading this book. So evaluate yourself. Is your procrastination rooted in rebellion, fear, or laziness? Face the cause and address it for what it is.

Each of us has areas where we are hesitant and unsure of ourselves. Planning and dealing with details are two things with which I have personally struggled. I love making presentations, but I hate writing speeches. When I waited to write a speech prior to scheduling the seminar, I never made a speech. Finally, I discovered what works for me. I picked a subject, entitled the seminar, scheduled it and then began inviting people...*Scary, huh?* Registrations started pouring in. I did not want to get in front of a crowd and tell them I did not have anything to say. So, it forced me to write the speech. Admittedly, my first few seminars were not perfect, but each one kept getting better. They never would have improved if I had not put myself in a predicament that forced me to move forward.

Procrastination is like driving in a rut down a gravel road. Someone has defined a *rut* as "a grave with one end knocked out." You cannot edge your way out of a rut. To get out of a rut, you have to make an abrupt turn. ***You have to decide that now, not later, you are going to do what you have been putting off.***

3-STEP PLAN FOR OVERCOMING PROCRASTINATION

FIRST STEP: Have a clear-cut objective.

One day, Charlie Brown was target-practicing with his bow and arrow. He shot an arrow and hit a wall, then drew a target around the arrow. He repeated this action by shooting trees, poles, and so on. Lucy inquired, "Charlie Brown, what are you doing?" He said, "Target practicing." She insisted, "Charlie Brown, that's **not** how you target practice. You have to draw the target first." Charlie responded, *"My way, I never miss!"*[2]

Choice is the beginning of all journeys. It has been said that the number one reason most people do not get what they want is that they do not know what they want.

You will never move from where you are until you decide that you would rather be somewhere else. Every achievement, both great and small, starts with a decision and continues with movement toward a goal.

SECOND STEP: Make a decision!

Procrastinating is the direct opposite of deciding. In a survey of 25,000 individuals that had failed in life, it was determined that a lack of decision was near the top of the list of thirty-one causes of failure.[3]

Decision comes from the Latin word *de* meaning "from" and *caedere* which means "to cut."[4] The term *deciduous*, as in *deciduous tree*, comes from this same Latin word. They are trees whose leaves *fall off* in autumn. A genuine decision suggests that something old must *fall off* or *be cut off* in order for the new to grow. Make a decision! Then cut yourself off from any possibility of failing. If something does not *fall away* as a direct result of your decision, then *you have not really made a decision*.

If you procrastinate and not make a decision, you have actually made a decision. You have decided not to decide. Why would you do that? It may suggest a lack of confidence that you can make the right decision. You might feel like things are out of control and that you are not in a position to make a decision. Either way, the underlying issue is fear of failure. You may not be sure of your decision, but indecision is sure to fail. Very young in my business career, I was managing a radio station. I was only twenty-two and had more ambition and spunk than knowledge and finesse. I hired a man by the name of Skip Tinnon to do part-time sports for me. Skip was probably twenty-five years older than me and was much wiser. I would call and give him an assignment, and he would tell me, "I will do something, even if it is wrong."

The one thing that never changes is that there will always be change. If you do not make a decision to change, you will be standing on the tracks someday and change will run over you like a freight train. So make a decision! Do something, even if it is wrong. Destiny is not a chance, but a choice!

THIRD STEP: Be willing to change.

I once saw a restaurant tip jar with the following sign: ***If you fear change, leave it here!*** Everyone may fear change to some degree. Mark Twain said, "I'm all for progress. It's change I object to."[5] Robert F. Kennedy wrote, "Progress is a nice word. But change is its motivator. And change has its enemies."[6] Alfred North Whitehead chimed in, "The art of progress is to preserve order amid change and to preserve change amid order."[7] Jim Rohn stated, "We generally change ourselves for one of two reasons: inspiration or desperation."[8]

Let's say that your Aunt Matilda died. That is bad news because you really liked her. She left you $3 million, and that is good news. However, you are a person that absolutely hates change and your life is about to change drastically. Once again, that is bad news. At last, the good news is that you can *give me* the $3 million and you do not have to worry about it. You will not have to change at all!

Although you may hate change, now you have three million reasons why change is not so bad. This example illustrates the reasoning process that everyone goes through when facing change. You weigh your dislike for change against the many positives that change may bring. In this case, the *money wins!* The *lesson* here is that we will only change when we perceive that the change is worth it!

BOTTOM LINE:

Do not make the process difficult. Just make a list of what needs to be done. Prioritize and do the most important things first. For each priority, choose what you least want to do and do it first to get it out of the way. Do not think about every task; just do the next task.

Chapter 5

Einstein
Syndrome

Do you have the *Einstein* Syndrome? This syndrome is at play in your life if your normal response to new situations is, "I am not doing anything until I know everything!" The key issue of the *Einstein* Syndrome is *perfectionism*.

Perfectionism is defined as an attitude or philosophy that demands perfection and rejects anything else. This syndrome is a first cousin to the *Mañana* Syndrome (that we looked at in chapter 4). Perfectionism also causes procrastination.

You reason, "I must do *this* before I can do *that*," or "As soon as I know exactly how this product works, I'll tell people about it." You convince yourself that it is okay *not* to make contacts until you know a little more about the products. Regrettably, you will *never* feel like you *know enough* to begin working. The truth is you are *wimping out!*

If you follow this thinking process for everything you do, you will never do anything. Sure, the concept sounds good: *information is power!* But it is not only impractical; it is impossible. Henry Ford invented the automobile which was sold by distributors. If distributors had avoided selling automobiles until they knew exactly how everything worked, we would still be riding around in horse-drawn buggies.

The *Einstein* Syndrome disregards anything short of perfection as unacceptable and a sign of personal worthlessness. When I read that definition, I think, *"Yikes!"* If everything has to be perfect before one can *go* ahead, one will never *get* ahead. Zig Ziglar said, "If you wait until all the lights are 'green' before you leave home, you'll never get started on your trip to the top."

If you think you have to know everything before you do anything, you are never going to get anything built. You will only get started at getting started. Yes, you need to understand what you are doing, but network marketing is an action and momentum business. You need to take action fast to get momentum. The pilot who flies a plane knows the basics of what makes it fly, but if he tried to learn how every little thing on the airplane worked, he would be too old to fly before he ever took off.

~ *Einstein* Syndrome ~

This syndrome happens more often with product knowledge. Those who market a nutritional product want to become nutritionists before they start marketing their product. Remember, this business is network marketing, not network "nutritioning." Yes, you need to know the basics of your product and how it works, but your job is marketing. So in the beginning, learn enough about your product to tell people what it does and how to use it. The longer you work with your company, the more you will learn about your products. It is just a natural transference.

Some people will hide themselves in product research so that they have an excuse for not getting out and doing the things that move product. This behavior can lead to *analysis paralysis!* The more you think about what you do not know, the more frozen you will become.

~Don't let what you *do not* know stop you from using what you *do* know!~

Instead of "Ready-Aim-Fire*,*" those affected by the *Einstein* Syndrome tend to get ready, then aim...aim...aim...aim...aim... (They never do fire the thing!) aim...aim...aim...aim! I play golf. I have noticed that the longer I stand over the ball and prepare to swing, the less likely it is to go anywhere close to where I want it to go.

You should learn all you can about your product, but get your marketing business going and pick up the technical knowledge as you go along. You need to know immediately what your product does; you can learn why it does it later. The truth is if you do not want to make contacts, you can always spend your time studying about your product. King Solomon said, "The slothful man says, 'There is a lion outside! I shall be slain in the streets!'" (Proverbs 22:13) If you are looking for an excuse to do nothing, there will always be lots of things to study. Certainly, you need to know what your product does so that you can explain the benefits, but how it does it can be picked up as you go along. Most of us would be in the dark if we had to know exactly how electricity works before we would turn on the lights.

A parked car is hard to steer! It is better to move in the wrong direction and get turned toward the right direction than it is just to sit there.

~ *Einstein* Syndrome ~

3-STEP PLAN FOR OVERCOMING PERFECTIONISM

FIRST STEP: Redefine your purpose for starting this business.

What is your *why*, your dream, your reason for building your business? Rewrite your goals. Visualize what your life will be like when you have reached those goals.

SECOND STEP: Decide to let yourself learn as you go.

Jim Rohn said, "Don't let your learning lead to knowledge. Let your learning lead to action!"[2] Successful people usually do not need one hundred percent of the information before making a decision. That would take too long and bog them down in their decision-making. At the risk of sounding overly simplistic, *just do it!* This mentality is shared by truly successful people.

~Don't make excuses, just make good!~

The truth is that anyone can do this business if they truly want to! You use a product and then refer it to other people who do the same. Do not make this job harder than it is. Your job is to make the contacts. If you can tell people about the movie you saw, the restaurant where you ate, and the shoes you just bought, then you can share this business, too.

THIRD STEP: Become an expert on the benefits of your product, not the mechanics of it.

Learn what your product will do for people and how best to use it in order to obtain the full benefit. Getting this knowledge usually takes much less time than becoming an expert on how the product works. Benefits are what people are really interested in anyway. They want to know how your product is going to improve their lives. They need to know how to use it to make it work. You should be able to learn this information in a matter of minutes. Many times, I have seen people get in a business that sells nutritional products and then think that they must become nutritionists to succeed. This mentality is a lose/lose scenario. It takes too much time away from you building your business and it intimidates others, making them feel that they, too, will have to become a nutritionist to become successful. So your whole business is slowed down, or even stopped, while everyone works on their doctorate degrees.

BOTTOM LINE:

Abraham had the testimony that he obeyed God. "[W]hen he was called to go out to the place which he would afterward receive as an inheritance...he went out, not knowing where he was going" (Hebrews 11:8). In other words, he went *going*, not *knowing*. He believed that he would be guided as he obeyed. He did not need to know everything first, and neither do you!

Chapter 6

Pass the Buck
Syndrome

Do you have the *Pass the Buck* Syndrome? President Harry Truman had a sign on his desk to remind him of the truth. The sign said, "The buck stops here."[1] If you find yourself saying or even thinking, "I can't get *anyone* to help me," or "I would succeed if I only had a good *mentor,*" or "My sponsor won't *help* me," you may have the *Pass the Buck* syndrome. These expressions are really just excuses for inactivity. You did not start your own business so that someone could make decisions for your future and take control of your life. You probably will not give others all the credit for your success, and you cannot blame them when you fail. The key issue of the *Pass the Buck* Syndrome is *taking ownership.*

The "I can't get any help!" rant can be translated, "My sponsor won't do it *for* me!" Perhaps, you have not yet crossed the bridge from *an employee mentality* to an *entrepreneur mentality*. People who own their business understand that even though outside factors affect their business, ultimately, failure or success is on their shoulders.

You will never get all you need from your sponsor or parent company. Up-line can be a big help, but if they did enough to build your business, they would not have time to build their own business, and then the whole system would break down.

There is an old saying: "If it is to *be*, it is up to *me*!"[2] This principle applies in every industry, especially network marketing. When you own your business, you buy the tools, pay your travel expenses, and purchase the marketing brochures to hand them out everywhere you go. You plan your work and work your plan. You make yourself go to work every day and take the good with the bad. You accept responsibility for becoming as efficient and effective as you can. Why? You do it because it is *your* business.

~ Pass the Buck Syndrome ~

3-STEP PLAN FOR TAKING OWNERSHIP

FIRST STEP: Learn to take responsibility for your own actions.

Teenagers tend to want the freedom of an adult, but rarely are ready for adult responsibility. Chances are one of the main reasons you started your business was the *freedom factor*. Freedom *will* come, but you usually have to wait until you build your business to a certain level of success. Unfortunately, responsibility comes immediately!

Let me repeat- this business is not brain surgery. If you have to, you can figure it out for yourself. Kill the mental pattern that always responds, "It's someone else's fault." This type of thinking suggests a *fear of punishment*, possibly rooted in early childhood. Those that struggle with this mindset can be caught with a *smoking gun* in hand; yet, they quickly declare it is *not* theirs. They have no clue how it arrived in their hands.

It is a personal choice as to whether you are a *victim* or a *victor*. It is time to stop being a *martyr* and go *make some money!* In short, ***grow up!***

SECOND STEP: Choose your freedoms and bondages.

Max E. Anders, in his book *Thirty Days to Understanding the Christian Life,* shares that with each freedom comes a cost. For instance, if you choose freedom from a toothbrush, you will inherit the bondage of tooth decay.[3] If you choose freedom from deodorant, you will realize the bondage of body order. If you choose the freedom of careless eating and no exercise, you may reap the bondage of ill health. If you choose the freedom of laziness, you may have to deal with the bondage of poverty. If you choose to buy whatever you want without adequate resources, then you will face the bondage of debt.

You must choose your freedoms and then live with the consequences. Conversely, you can choose the bondage of good planning, hard work, and diligent networking, and reap the freedom of time, money, and friends.

THIRD STEP: Remember that your business will not grow until *you* do!

To change your *outer* world, you must change your *inner* world. If you want different *fruit,* put down different *roots.* First change your *invisible* world, and then your *visible* world will change.

~ *Pass the Buck* Syndrome ~

Choose to invest in yourself. Read books. Listen to tapes. Talk to successful people and ask questions. Attend meetings, events, and conferences.

Capture positive thoughts on paper. Don't just think it, *ink it!* Write down affirmations and reasons why you *can* succeed in your business. Keep a journal and keep track of anything that motivates you. Review your journal often.

BOTTOM LINE:

Recognize that it is not your sponsor's responsibility to build your business. It is **yours**! Choose to make *your* business fly, no matter what it takes. Your sponsor already did the most important thing someone can do for anyone in networking by introducing you to the business. The better a sponsor leads, the better his or her business will be, but you are the master and commander of your business! Yes, you can be successful, but **you** have to go and make it happen!

Part II

Winning Habits

A wise person was once asked what it took to be successful. His insightful response was simply, *"Continue doing what works and stop doing what doesn't work!"* Aristotle said, "We are what we repeatedly do." Excellence is not an act, but a habit. It is true that we make our habits, and then our habits make us. This section deals with healthy habits that eventually produce success.

The following are some initial suggestions to consider:

1.) *A word to the wise:* If you are going to make a lot of money in networking, learn how to talk comfortably and confidently to people over the telephone. I have never met a top money earner that did not use the phone as a major tool in his or her business. Frankly, I prefer to talk to people in person. I like people and enjoy meeting them face to face. Nonetheless, I have learned to utilize the phone as an invaluable tool in my business. You should still make contacts in person, but the phone is very efficient. I can talk to four people over the phone in less time than it takes to meet with one person. So accept the phone and learn to appreciate its efficiency. On the other hand, meeting in person may be your forte, and you should not give that up. Time in person is very persuasive and will build relationships faster. You simply must learn to do both. Learn to balance your business.

2.) Never prejudge a person's potential. It is your job to introduce them to the opportunity. What they can or will do with it is up to them. I have recruited people that I knew could build a huge business and watched them do nothing. Others whose success seemed unsure to me built huge businesses. Besides, you never know when someone will lead you to a top producer. Never decide for someone else. No matter how successful or unsuccessful people are, share your business with them and let them decide what they will do with it.

3.) Every night sit down and make a list of three to six things that you want to accomplish the next day. Prioritize the list by order of importance. Many times, the hardest thing will be the most significant. The next morning, resolve to *eat the frog* and do the most important thing first. The remainder of your day will be a breeze. Also, determine how many contacts you will make each day and go to work to accomplish it. Then, before going to bed each night, write in your journal the answer to three key questions:

- What did I do well today?
- What do I need to improve next time?
- How will I make those improvements?

Chapter 7

Superman
Syndrome

We are all familiar with the story of Superman- the man of steel, faster than a speeding bullet, more powerful than a locomotive, able to leap tall buildings in a single bound. We also know that when he is not doing his gig as Superman, he is mild-mannered reporter Clark Kent, cleverly disguised in a pair of black glasses. Many times, I have seen people get into networking and immediately start telling their friends and relatives they are going to be rich. They have started a networking business, and their friends should join them so that they can be rich as well.

What you are saying to your friends is that all of your life you have been mild-mannered, regular Joe or Jill, but you have now taken off your glasses, entered a phone booth, and become Super

Network Marketer. You are not only going to be rich yourself, but you are going to help them get rich too.

I love the enthusiasm, but nobody was really fooled by Clark's glasses. We just pretend we do not recognize him. When you approach your friends and family with a first-time dream to build a huge networking business, you are asking them to pretend you are now a different person. If you have been a secretary for years, they see you as a successful secretary, but not a successful networker. If you have been an engineer, they see you as a capable engineer, but not a capable networker that they can trust to lead them into success.

I have seen many people get discouraged because their friends and family do not take their networking business seriously. The truth is that you do not necessarily have bad friends and family. You just may be approaching them the wrong way.

3-STEP PLAN FOR
CURING THE *SUPERMAN* SYNDROME

FIRST STEP: Get help with your first contacts.

Do not start telling people about the business until you know something about it. Let your up-line and the business tools share the business with your personal warm market (friends and relatives). The principle is similar to that in Christianity- you are not the message, just the messenger.

SECOND STEP: Learn how to use the tools of the trade.

So how do you motivate a person to talk to your up-line, attend an event, or participate in a webinar or conference call? How do you get them to listen to a CD or watch a DVD? You have to learn how to properly promote those tools. One of the most important skills in networking is *edification*, which means making the people in your up-line sound so good that others will want to talk to them and listen to or watch their recordings. Your potential business candidates will see that they do not have to be experts because there is an expert already there to help them. Until you have built a business, your own peers cannot see you as a networking expert. They can, however, recognize the talents of someone they do not know but whom you have promoted as an expert, which will give them the confidence to step out. Also, when you edify your up-line, your down-line learns to edify you.

THIRD STEP: Keep the right goal in mind when talking with people.

Realize you are not trying to sell this business to people. Rather, you are looking for those who are interested in the lifestyle made available by building a business. You do not want to persuade; you want to inform. Your goal is to get them to see the plan and understand what is possible if they choose to become involved. So do not try to get them to do it. Get them to look at it and let them decide. Accept their decision. If you do not push them now, they may come around later.

BOTTOM LINE:

You cannot do this business by yourself. It is called "networking," not "me-working." If you have to do everything yourself, your people will assume the same for themselves, and you will not duplicate. Learn to use, promote, and edify your tools and business partners.

Chapter 8

Saddling Up
Syndrome

We discovered long ago that it is easier and more comfortable to put a saddle on a horse than it is to just jump on and ride him bareback. Saddling up does slow the process, but it is usually worth it. Good preparation is generally a good time investment. The *Saddling Up* Syndrome is a problem when all of your time is spent getting ready to do something and very little of your time is spent actually doing it. If you go by a Starbucks at five o'clock in the morning, you will probably find the lights on and people in the shop stocking shelves, setting up the cash register, and sweeping the floor. They are there working, but the doors are locked. No one can get any coffee. Then about five or ten minutes before 6 a.m., the employees will start brewing coffee. At six o'clock, they will open the doors and let the customers in. They will be open all day, and then at about 10 p.m., they will lock the doors. There will still be people working, but they are not taking business. They are counting the money, cleaning up, closing down, and getting ready for the next day. They will probably all be gone in an hour or so.

What if the Starbucks employees did it differently? What if at six in the morning, they did not open the doors? What if they just kept getting ready? What if they arranged and rearranged the stock over and over just to get it perfect? Then at seven o'clock, they thought about opening, but realized the coffee was old by then and they must re-brew. The floor is not as clean as it could be, so they mop it again. The cookies could be displayed better, so they are moved. What if this went on and on all day? People would come to the door, shake it, and find it locked. They would look in and somebody who works there would holler out, "We are not ready yet! Come back later!" Then, finally, a couple of hours before closing, when most of the customers have gone somewhere else, they open the doors and let people in. That is pretty silly, isn't it? They would go broke and be closed in weeks, maybe days. Even Starbucks could not sustain such a poor business practice.

Any successful business will always spend the overwhelming proportion of time open, rather than closed for preparation to do business. Many retail stores today do not close at all. They keep their doors open twenty-four hours a day and do their preparation

~ *Saddling Up* Syndrome ~

overnight when the customer flow is much slower. It is the only rational way to do business. They know they are never going to ride the horse if all they do is saddle up.

The *Saddling Up* Syndrome in networking is when the largest portion of your time is spent getting ready to talk to people, and only a small portion of your time is spent actually being in front of people, making contacts, and presenting your business. Look at your last two-week calendar. Retrace your time. Was more time spent getting ready to talk to people or actually talking to people? In networking the only time your doors are open is when you are recruiting and helping other people to recruit. Just as Starbucks would not succeed if they spent eighty percent of their time getting ready to open and only twenty percent of their time open to the public, so your business will not succeed if you do not keep your doors open more than you prepare to open them.

3-STEP PLAN FOR
CURING THE *SADDLING UP* SYNDROME

FIRST STEP: Keep a calendar and write down your activity during your work time.

Distinguish what you do during that time and how much is spent with your doors open (recruiting and helping others recruit.) Evaluate how you are using your time.

SECOND STEP: Choose the tools you are normally going to use for recruiting and trust them to be good enough.

Do not spend all of your time tweaking everything. Use the tools offered you by your company and up-line. Do not try to create your own. Until you have reached a level in your company that allows you to enjoy a very comfortable income, you should be using tools, not creating them.

THIRD STEP: Operate on an 80/20 rule.

Eighty percent of your time is spent recruiting and helping others recruit, and twenty percent of your time is spent preparing to recruit. If you want to stay open twenty-four hours a day, listen to CDs, MP3s, and webinars while you are doing other things.

~ *Saddling Up* Syndrome ~

Always take new recruits with you to training sessions. Always include prospects on conference calls and webinars. Always have a prospect with you for every opportunity meeting. Make it a goal to never attend opportunity meetings or training meetings alone.

BOTTOM LINE:

You must spend the bulk of your business time recruiting and helping others recruit. Recruiting is like removing a huge rock from the middle of the road. It takes momentum and demands a huge effort just to get it to budge a little. If you push long enough with sustained force, the rock will move a few inches forward and then backward. Once it begins to rock, you can eventually get it to roll. At that point, you just steady it along and push it out of the way. However, if the rock comes to a complete stop too soon, you must repeat the entire process to get it moving again.

If your doors are not open, your business cannot grow. TheyABS are only open when you are recruiting or helping someone in your down-line recruit. ***Keep your doors open!***

Chapter 9

Missing Link
Syndrome

*I*n 1991, Billy Crystal and Jack Palance made a movie called *City Slickers*. It is a comedy about some friends from the city who take a vacation on a dude ranch. Curly, played by Jack Palance, is a rough, old cowboy who works on the ranch, and Billy Crystal is the city slicker learning to be a cowboy. He becomes Billy Crystal's role model and mentor. Curly repeatedly holds up his index finger and says to Billy, "There's one thing, one thing. You have to know the one thing."[1]

In networking if you do not discover that "one thing" there will always be a "missing link," and you are never going to make any real money. You are going to be frustrated and discouraged. Or even worse, you may become satisfied to accept only a fraction of the success that is available to you. The missing link, or one thing, is that this business is about recruiting other business partners and not just about sales. If you recruit properly, you will be selling the product. If you only talk about the product but not the business opportunity, you will not create enough momentum to build a successful business. Today's networking is about building a network of business partners who love and use the products, but their main goal is to build a business.

Naturally, we need to have customers, but that is the by-product of the recruiting process. You can use your time to sell product and hope to find a few others who also want to sell product, and over a long period of time you can make a modest part-time income. Or you can spend your time recruiting business partners who will spend their time recruiting business partners, and you can build a huge income. Selling product is adding customers to your business. Recruiting business partners is multiplying customers to your business. If you find a new customer today, that is good. You have one new customer. If you find just a customer, it usually ends there. However, if you find a new distributor who is a business builder, you also have a customer who may find another customer tomorrow who, in turn, may find a new customer, and so on.

I hope this explanation gives you an "ah ha!" moment. If you want to help more people with your product, you need to find more people who want to build a business because that will find customers who find customers, rather than you just finding a

~ *Missing Link* Syndrome ~

customer. It is simple. Find distributors who want to build a business, not just use the product, and you will multiply your product sales. You find who you look for. If you are talking just about the product, you will find product-users. If you are talking about building a business and making money, you will find business partners who will find other business partners and multiply your business.

You probably should read the previous paragraphs again. All of the big money earners in networking have huge down-lines of distributors—not some of the big money earners, ***all*** of the big money earners. It is the leverage of a lot of distributors who do a small amount of sales (mostly to themselves) and a lot of recruiting of other business partners that give a person the big money and the time and freedom that draw people to networking in the first place. Recruiting distributors who are business-builders is the key issue in overcoming the *Missing Link* Syndrome.

3-STEP PLAN FOR
RECRUITING BUSINESS PARTNERS

FIRST STEP: Learn to frame your product as a business.

I know we all love our products and want to tell people about them. However, as you speak with people, I want to ask you to wait just twenty seconds to talk about the product and first frame it as a business.

You are going to run into people that need your product. First, identify the problem. Then, rather than saying, "You need to get this product to solve your problem," try saying something like the following: "It is interesting that you have this problem. I am associated with a company that has developed a product that has been very successful at solving that problem. As a matter of fact, it has been so successful that it has created fortunes for many of those who had the foresight to help introduce this product to the market. Would you like more information about this company and its product?" Now, they are going to ask you for the information, rather than you pushing it on them.

Remember, first impressions last. If you just share the product, they will always see you as a product peddler. If you first frame it as a business, you still get to tell them about the product and how it will solve their problem. However, by waiting twenty seconds and sharing the big picture, they will see you as a business person.

SECOND STEP: Obtain the right recruiting tools.

If you keep making recruiting your top priority, you will succeed! Set up your business so that you can look for new distributors *every day*. If you are beginning your business, you will need the following tools:

- A *computer* with internet access. You also need an *email address*.

- I normally recommend a *wireless telephone.* Why? You should not be locked to one location; you need to be free to move around. Some people may work better in one location at a desk or office, and a wired phone works for them. That is fine, but you are going to need a phone that you do not mind using.

- *Three-way calling* on your phone. Remember you are on a team. This feature will give you the ability to connect a prospect with someone up-line. Three-way calling on a land line phone is a must and is simple to use. If you are going to use a cell phone for your business calls, you must make sure that the three-way calling function is simple to use and that you know how to use it. You may have to switch cell phones to find one with a simple three-way function.

- *Unlimited long distance.* Some of your best prospects may live out of town.

- *A headset.* It is more comfortable when you spend a lot of time on the phone. You need one with a mute button so that you can maximize freedom and, when necessary, minimize noise.

- The best tool is the one that works for you. It is the tool that you will use. Avoid anything *uncomfortable* because you will not use it for very long.

- *CDs, DVDs, recordings, brochures & websites.* Your up-line will recommend these tools. Do not try to create your own; use the proven tools.

What a wonderful business! With just a telephone and internet access you can build an international business.

Note: Informational technology is changing so quickly that it is impossible to predict the tools that will be available (even at the time of publishing this book).

THIRD STEP: Get on the system and find prospects through it.

If you are new to networking, your company and up-line, no doubt, have some kind of system for recruiting. Get on track and follow their system. Do not try to create your own. There are three markets for finding prospects: *warm market, meet market,* and *cold market.*

The first is the *warm market.* This market is your *center of influence*, consisting of friends and family. These are individuals with which you already have a current, viable, working relationship. Your center of influence can also include acquaintances (people you know or those who know you). Never prejudge their interest. Share the business and let them decide for themselves.

The *meet market* involves people that you casually meet every day. You strike up a conversation with someone and then exchange contact information. Once you get a phone number and/or email address, you can contact the person to see if he or she has further interest.

Another area is the *cold market.* This market entails advertising to people that you have never met. Here you are *not* dependent on family and friends and you will never run out of people. Although it may be more difficult, a cold market is better than no market at all. Most people should not start advertising independently. Successful advertising is a skill that takes experience. Experience is a great teacher, but the tuition is very high. If you are going to advertise, it is best to be part of an advertisement co-op sponsored by your up-line or a professional in the industry. When choosing to advertise, you should set an advertisement budget just like traditional businesses do. Set a budget in which you can spend money on a regular basis while staying within its limits. Also, choose a budget that does not put you into debt. If you cannot afford to pay for it in advance, you should not be spending money on it. Advertising takes time, but it does work. It can be a great tool in your business, but you must be cautious and avoid getting in over your head.

~It is important that you never stop recruiting!~

Success in your networking business is not magic. It is like any other business. You build a clientele and get paid a portion of the sales price. The more you sell, the more you make—it is *that* simple.

You cannot control results, but you can control activity. As discussed previously in the first chapter, "whatever a man sows, that he will also reap….And let us not grow weary while doing good, for in due season we shall reap if we do not lose heart" (Galatians 6:7, 9).

If you are a networking professional, remember that *your group will do what you do.* If you recruit, they will recruit! If you stop recruiting, they will stop recruiting!

Never take a vacation from recruiting. This issue is very common among mid-level network marketers. They say, "I don't have time to recruit. I have to support my group." If it has been

~ *Missing Link* Syndrome ~

a while since you have recruited someone or your business is slowing down, then you may have lost valuable momentum.

BOTTOM LINE:

Never lose momentum by failing to enlist new distributors! It is like pushing a very heavy ball uphill. If you stop pushing it before you get to the top, the ball does not just sit there, but starts to roll back down. Stopping the fall and starting to move forward again is much more work than keeping up a consistent effort toward reaching your goals.

Chapter 10

Hobby Syndrome

Do you have the *Hobby* Syndrome? You tell everyone that you are building a business, but you treat it like a hobby. You work when it is convenient and do not keep regular business hours. The key issue to the *Hobby* Syndrome is *commitment*.

I like to golf. But if it is raining, I do not play. Why? It is my hobby, not my profession. When it is convenient, I am always ready for a round of golf, but I refuse to be uncomfortable. I have not made a dime playing golf. In fact, golf costs me a lot of money. I do not complain because I understand it is just a hobby.

The same is true for those who play football in the vacant lot with their buddies on Saturday afternoon. They play football, but they are not football players. Real football players practice and work out every day. For those in the lot, it is a hobby, a relaxing pastime, a fun activity.

When building a business, it will be *inconvenient* at times, and you will feel very *uncomfortable*. You may visualize your personal success in network marketing and live in a *Disney World* of imagination much of the time. Unfortunately, you cannot just sit there envisioning your success and make money. At some point, you have to *get up, get going, and get out there!*

~ "Man stands for long time with mouth open before roast duck flies in." – Chinese Proverb~

Ann Landers wrote, "Opportunities are usually disguised as hard work."[1] Albert Einstein proclaimed, "Vision without execution is hallucination."[2] Thomas Edison suggested, "Good things come to those who wait, but only those things left by those who hustle."[3] Saint Jerome in the fourth century wrote, "I like work; it fascinates me. I can sit and look at it for hours." Will Rogers said, "Even if you're on the right track, you will get run over if you just sit there."[4]

~"For a dream comes through much activity"

– Ecclesiastes 5:3a~

Socrates stated, "Let him that would move the world, first move himself."[8] Solomon also said, "Where no oxen are, the

~ *Hobby* Syndrome ~

[feed] trough is clean, but much increase comes by the strength of an ox" (Proverbs 14:4). It is not always easy working with people. We are in the *people business*! There will always be conflict and emotional messes. One pastor suggested that sheep bite! It is the nature of the beast. Do not let people scare you into inactivity!

So how can you tell if you have a business or a hobby? One way to diagnose the *Hobby* Syndrome is to count the number of contacts you made last week. If you can count them on one hand, you have been afflicted.

If your networking business is a hobby, then you will not have the commitment to do what it takes to make it happen. When it is not convenient, you will not work. However, if you are building a legitimate networking business, then you need to determine how many contacts it will take to succeed. Ask yourself how many hours you need to work and if you are willing to make that commitment.

If you treat your business like a hobby, it will pay you like a hobby. It is sheer fantasy to think you do not have to work hard and still be paid like a CEO or rock star.

3-STEP PLAN FOR WORKING HARD

FIRST STEP: Commit to Minimum Daily Contacts (MDCs).

Set a goal of making at least five contacts per day. In fact, many successful distributors have a goal of five to ten contacts per day. Set regular workdays, no less than three days per week. No business can succeed without regular hours.

One technique that has helped many people involves a bag of beans. Put five or ten beans in your left pocket every morning. Every time you make a contact, move a bean to your right pocket. Your daily goal is to move all of the beans from one pocket to the other. Do not stop until it is done!

You may need MWCs (Minimum Weekly Contacts) as a goal. That is okay. Just be faithful to your commitment.

SECOND STEP: Keep a record of your contacts.

~If you do not keep records, you probably will not break any!~

Ernest Hemingway arose early every morning before sunrise most of his adult life. He wrote every day. Afterward, he counted the number of words and charted it on a wall. Throughout the day, that number either applauded or indicted him.[5]

~ *Hobby* Syndrome ~

If you do not keep records, it is very easy to think that you are making more contacts than you are. Remember that building any kind of business will be *hard* if you work at it *easy,* but it will be *easy* if you work at it *hard.*

THIRD STEP: Have an accountability partner.

The world's greatest principle of management is—People will not do what you *expect*, but what you *inspect!*

Assign someone to become your accountability partner, and give him or her permission to ask you the tough question each week: "How many contacts have you made…*really?!?"*

BOTTOM LINE:
The only way to cure the *Hobby* Syndrome is to work your business like a job. Commit to making a certain number of contacts on a daily or weekly basis and then show up for work. Do not let distractions take priority over your business. If you are not making contacts, you are not building your business. You can eavesdrop on all of the conference calls. You can listen to all of the training until you can teach it yourself. You can go to all of the meetings. Even so, if you are not making the contacts, you are not going to make any money! The truth is that your

group is going to do what you do, so set a good example. Turn your vision into a venture, and *take action today!*

Chapter 11

Rescue Mission
Syndrome

Do you have the *Rescue Mission* Syndrome? When you talk about the price of your products, does your throat strangely tighten? Do you over-compensate by giving away lots of product to family and friends? Your rationale is that they cannot afford it, so you will buy it for them. The key issue of the *Rescue Mission* Syndrome is *belief in product value*.

Do you realize that the majority of people to whom you give product will not use it anyway? They take it solely because you want to give it to them, not because they actually want to try it. To avoid confrontation or offense, they accept the product. Then, they throw it away or pour it out. If you want someone to use the product more than they want to use it, you are probably wasting the gift. They will look for excuses not to like it. They buy the other things they need and want in life, and, if they really wanted it, they would buy your product, too!

People who want the product but cannot afford it should become distributors and earn enough to pay for their own products. In most cases, the tax deductions alone are enough to more than pay for the products of most distributors. You work for your money to buy products. Why should you also have to work to pay for others' products?

Every rule has an exception. If you can afford it, then giving product to a family member or friend that would truly appreciate it may work for you. But do not count it as a business cost since it is a charitable act by you and should not be part of evaluating the success of your business.

In certain circumstances, it may be advantageous to give away a trial-size portion, but never give away more than a month's worth of product. Even then, I rarely recommend it. Give people only enough for a good test and tell them, "I'm giving this product to you as a gift to try. If you're happy with it, then I'll show you how you can order it for yourself on a regular basis." Do not give it to them in such an open-ended way that they assume you will always buy it for them.

I have seen distributors give away product and it actually hurt their business. It also makes your business less profitable. I have seen people give away product while trying to build a business, and after a year they look at the inflated cost and get incredibly discouraged.

Giving away product that is *not* trial-size is an activity that cannot be easily duplicated. If you give someone product and they become a distributor, he or she will assume that they must also give away product to build their business. It may hinder them from continuing.

Since most companies offer a money-back guarantee, every new purchase is a trial purchase. Consumers can get their money back if they do not like the product.

3-STEP PLAN FOR
PROTECTING YOUR PRODUCT

FIRST STEP: Understand that people make choices.

People can afford whatever they prioritize in life. They can afford cable TV, rent videos, and eat all the junk food they want. If they really want the product, they will find a way to buy it.

Do not feel guilty charging your friends and family for product. Hopefully, they are paying the rest of their bills, and they should buy this product, too.

SECOND STEP: Understand that you are providing premium products.

Come to grips with the fact that the products are *worth it.* It is worth it to you, to your group, and to your friends and family. Compare your product with the price of poor health or unhealthy home and personal care products.

You have to be convinced to be convincing. You must be convinced that your product is a good value. It does not have to be the cheapest. The cheapest product is almost never the best value. Persuaded people are persuasive, which is an important principle to pass on to your group.

It is like the difference between a Rolls Royce and a Chevy. The Chevy costs much less than the Rolls Royce, but it does not mean it is a better value. The Rolls will always have a value; the Chevy will most likely eventually end up in the junk yard. Remember, you are providing value. Leave the discounting to Wal-Mart. By the way, when was the last time you received anything free at Wal-Mart? People expect to pay for what they get, unless you train them differently. When was the last time Wal-Mart sent you a check for referring people to them?

THIRD STEP: Understand that if you will build your business now, you will eventually be able to give away anything you want later.

If you want to give product away, then make so much money that it will not be a *burden*. *Jesus said that "the poor will be with you always"* (Matthew 26:11). There will always be individuals to whom you can give. You want your loved ones to have product because you know it will help them. Then make a *lot of money* and give it to them with no strings attached when money is no longer an issue.

BOTTOM LINE:

When people question the price of the product, deal with it up front. I tell them, "If you think they are too high priced, prove it to me and try it for thirty days. If you don't think the product is worth every penny you paid for it, you can get your money back." Be assured that the products are so good and deliver so well that they will never let you down.

Chapter 12

Jack-in-the-Box
Syndrome

Do you have the *Jack-in-the-Box* Syndrome? When you pop out and try to light up the world, is there always someone there to hit you on the head and shove you back in the box. Are you easily brought down to the level of those around you? When you see the future brighter than your friends, do they call you a *dreamer?* Are they constantly challenging your optimistic view of life? This syndrome may be at play if you are not permitted to *think big* without penalty of persecution. The key issue of the *Jack-in-the-Box* Syndrome is *wrong or limiting associations.*

The Jack-in-the-Box Syndrome happens often in adult life. You realize that you have been stuck in a box of limited thinking. Something or someone *trips your trigger* and you bounce out of this box, only to discover that not everyone delights in your newfound liberty. Instantly, family and friends attempt to put you back in your place. They are more comfortable with you in the box, and they want to keep you there.

One would think that those who love you the most would be thrilled with your advancement, but that is certainly *not* always the case! Most people do not like change! If you are changing, it makes others nervous because you might expect them to change, too. It seems easier just to keep you down than it would be to climb out of their boxes. They love you and mean well, and from their limited view they think they are protecting you. Yet, they really need to be encouraging you.

The U.S. Small Business Administration website declares that the number one reason businesses fail is because of advice (or investment which generates advice) from friends and relatives. Normally, it is advice from people who have no expertise or experience that influence the decisions of their loved ones. Sometimes, the advice is based in jealousy. Other times, the advice is sincere; they are simply trying to protect you. Either way, if you let the judgment of others come between you and your dreams, you will be robbed of what might have been.

If you go fishing in a gulf or an ocean and catch only one blue crab, you will need to put a lid on the bucket or it will escape. However, if you catch two or more, there is no need for a lid and they will remain captured. Instead of pulling together, when one blue crab tries to climb out, another one will grab it and pull it down. One is trapped by the fear and ignorance of the others, and all of them become better known as...*dinner!*

Some individuals who are content with their lot in life are more comfortable if their associations are at the same level. They may resent the fact that someone is trying to *get out of the bucket that they call home.* It makes them feel better if others share the *status quo.*

~Someone has said that s*tatus quo* is Latin for *"the mess we're in!"*[1]~

If a mountain lion attacks a small herd of horses, the horses by instinct form a circle, put their heads together, and begin kicking out against their mutual adversary. When donkeys are assaulted, they form a circle facing the mountain lion and kick each other. Time is too short to be kicking each other! Associate with those willing to *put their heads together* and move ahead. Otherwise, you will be just another jack...you know what I mean.

3-STEP PLAN FOR AVOIDING WRONG ASSOCIATIONS

FIRST STEP: Recognize four different types of people in your life.

Identify those that *add* to your life. In nearly every conversation with these individuals, there is something said that enhances, encourages, or empowers you in some way. Solomon wisely stated, "As iron sharpens iron, so a man sharpens the countenance of his friend" (Proverbs 17:7). Find people that sharpen you, even if the *sparks fly!* Cherish those that add to you! Creatively find time to be around them.

Discern those that *subtract* from your life. These individuals always need something from you. We are quick to say that these people are not bad, nor should we avoid them. Remember that life is a balancing act of *good and bad, give and take.* There may be days when you will *add* to others and other days when you will *take.* Such is life! The problem lies in relationships where one is always *giving* and the other is always *taking.* It is not wrong that people subtract from you unless they are *always* taking from you.

Appreciate those that *multiply* you. These individuals compensate for your weaknesses, and together you can accomplish great things. You were not meant to walk through life alone. Carefully select those that will walk closest with you.

~ *Jack-in-the-Box* Syndrome ~

One Belgium work horse can pull four tons, but two horses, after learning how to pull together, can pull twelve-and-a-half tons. That is a staggering one-half increase! Team up with those that will multiply (and not merely add to) your efforts!

Spot those that *divide* your success. These are individuals that (if you let them) will diminish your achievements. They are *emotional vampires* that suck precious energy from you. Avoid people who are constantly putting you down. If you cannot avoid the *dividers*, like family members or employers, at least do not talk to them about your business. Keep your conversations on subjects that do not lead to conflict.

Samson, the strong man from the Bible, was not wise to hang out with Delilah. She appeared to love him, but felt she could better herself by bringing him down. He eventually shared the secret of his strength: He had taken a Nazarite vow and his unusual power was connected to his long hair. She cut his hair while he slept, and stole his strength.

Be aware of those individuals that try to *cut your hair;* they will steal your strength! You can live with these people; just do not share your dreams and goals with them. It is better that way for everyone involved.

SECOND STEP: Proactively invest your time in those that add or multiply you!

Find positive people that share your goals, and spend time with them. Attend the meetings, events, and conventions that are held by your up-line and company. You should never miss an opportunity to be with people that have obtained the goals you seek.

When you are with these people, listen and ask questions. Too many times, I have seen people who have a dream get with someone who has achieved it, and instead of listening and learning from that person, they are continually trying to impress this potential mentor with what they are doing. You already know what you are doing. You need to find out what successful people did to get them where they are.

THIRD STEP: Learn to stand on your own feet.

No one was anywhere near the level of Jesus of Nazareth. He was pretty much a lone eagle. Even his own followers were constantly barraging him with unbelief. He had an inner knowledge of the true reality that anything is possible if one only has faith. Jesus walked on water and fed five thousand people with a mere five loaves of bread and two fish. He healed the sick and raised the dead. If he needed money for taxes, he called it from the sea. Truly, nothing was impossible for him! He did not allow the unbelief of his disciples to stop him. In fact, he lifted his disciples to a new level of faith.

If you are going to reach big goals, then you will eventually have to become the successful person others seek to be with—the immovable, determined, confident leader that helps himself or herself by helping others. So decide to be that person now. Determine in your heart that you will be successful. Look into your imagination and see yourself successful. Force yourself to think and talk successfully and positively. The sooner you can walk on your own, the sooner you will be able to soar with the eagles.

BOTTOM LINE:

You are either going to be the influencer or the influenced. There will always be someone around you who will tell you it cannot be done. You must take responsibility for your own destiny and avoid letting the unbelief of others steal your dream.

Chapter 13

Lone Ranger Syndrome

When I was a kid, my brothers and I loved to watch *The Lone Ranger*. Actually, he was never alone because he always had Tonto nearby. Of course, Tonto was not a ranger, so I guess he could qualify as being the Lone Ranger. Basically, he had to get rid of bad guys without the help of other rangers. He was the only one. Tonto could hang around, but we never forgot which one was the ranger.

Some people in networking have the *Lone Ranger* Syndrome. They have to do everything themselves. They do not ask for help from up-line or enlist the talents of down-line. They want to go it alone and do everything themselves. They never call up-line: *don't need 'em!* They have no time to introduce new distributors to others, and show zero interest in conducting training calls or attending events (unless they are in charge).

They revel in being self-made people. The key issue of the *Lone Ranger* Syndrome is *pride.*

"It's not pride," you say. "I'm self-reliant." But it is either pride or, worse yet, you do not know you need help. It is hard to help someone who does not think he or she needs it. Even if you actually do not need any help with your business, you demonstrate a principle to your down-line that if they are to be true leaders like you, they must also do it themselves. Now let's get real. How could you possibly build a network by yourself? The term *network* denotes more than just you. No one has ever done anything really significant by themselves.

In the past, when I have heard someone say they were *self-made*, I could not resist from inquiring, "How did that go for you when you were six months old changing your own diapers? Wasn't that difficult fixing your own lunch at age one?" My point—all of us *depend* upon others at various times in life.

The American poet John Donne wrote, "No man is an island."[1] The Apostle Paul said, "For none of us lives to himself, and no one dies to himself" (Romans 14:7). Solomon informed us that "[t]wo are better than one, because they have a good reward for their labor. For if they fall, one will lift up his companion. But woe to him who is alone when he falls, for he has no one to help him up" (Ecclesiastes 4:9-10).

Stephen Brown in his book, *Follow the Wind,* shares a witty story about teamwork. A long time ago, a man was driving in the country when his car slid off into a ditch. He desperately tried to get it unstuck, but he could not do it. He walked to the nearest farm, shared his plight, and asked for help. The old farmer responded, "I only have one mule, Dusty, and he's blind. I don't know if he can do it, but we'll try." Dusty was led down the road and hooked up to the car. Then the farmer yelled, "Pull, you mules! Go Dusty, Sammy, and Billy!" Sure enough, Dusty pulled the car right out of the ditch. The stranded motorist thanked the farmer profusely and then inquired, "Why did you call out the names of other mules when you only had Dusty?" "Oh," said the farmer, *"Dusty could have never done it if he thought he had to do it by himself."*[2]

~When you do everything yourself, it makes your down-line feel that they, too, should do everything themselves lest they be considered weak.~

An old Rabbi saying states, "He who goes alone very far, goes mad!"[3] In networking especially, separating yourself from your group is a crazy thing to do.

Synergy is "combined action or functioning." A more sophisticated definition is "the interaction of elements that when combined produce a total effect that is greater than the sum of the individual elements."[4] Simply put, it means 2+2=5. When you work together as a team, you will accomplish more than individuals merely working in a group. Ken Blanchard said,

"The mantra today is none of us is as smart as all of us."[5] Ray Kroc, founder of McDonalds, declared, "No one of us is more important than the rest of us."[6]

Synergy is easily illustrated in sports. Basketball great, Michael Jordan, once scored a remarkable sixty-four points in a game and they *still lost*.[7] Why? They did not play as a team. Did you know that a team of ten to fifteen mountain climbers tied to one another can absorb the fall of one climber? If there were only a few climbers, the fallen climber would yank the rest off of the mountain.

It is easy to recognize the *Lone Ranger* Syndrome because a lone ranger will try to keep his or her group isolated. "Don't call my group," one will say, "That is my job." Instead of helping the down-line to develop relationships with the up-line, a lone ranger hinders it and wants to be perceived as the sole leader of the group. This type of person is trying to build a cult, not a network. Cults are very unhealthy and usually small because a cult cannot grow past the leader. Since this person has a flawed perspective, nothing good usually happens. The leader of a cult must convince the small flock that he or she alone has the truth. With the communication tools available in today's society, that is pretty hard to do. People start to question in their minds what is right, and will eventually do nothing.

3-STEP PLAN FOR CURING THE *LONE RANGER* SYNDROME

FIRST STEP: Understand what happens when you do not work as a team.

It is true that a person with this syndrome can successfully sponsor people and move product. However, serious problems will surface down the road. In networking, whatever one does, whether good or bad, is duplicated. So the lone ranger creates a small network of lone rangers who are all trying to do it themselves. At some point, a lone ranger gets tired of trying to do all of the work that was meant to be leveraged through the up-line. Growth is stunted and moves slowly due to the lack of that leverage, and the lone ranger stops working.

As each lone ranger exits, the fledgling group is left to fend for itself. The habit of *not* working together by calling on the up-line has already been embedded in new distributors' thinking. In time, they too feel isolated and become discouraged. The entire down-line eventually withers away.

SECOND STEP: Plug in and get your people plugged in to the system.

Get involved in the meetings, events, conference calls, webinars, and web streamings that are sponsored by your up-line and company. Get your people to do the same. Events and meetings will be an essential part of your success.

You have heard the statement repeatedly, "Believe and achieve." It is equally true that if you *don't* believe, you *won't* achieve! That is why it is important to be surrounded by a support group that believes in you and your product. To offset all negatives, create a culture of positives around you. Being plugged in with others who believe is always helpful. Faith multiplies in groups.

You and your group need to hear the successes of others. In the movie *The Edge* with Anthony Hopkins and Alec Baldwin, the men were stranded in the Northern Wilderness and stalked by a grizzly bear with no weapon except a pocket knife. Hopkins's character had read how another man had killed a bear with a homemade spear, so he decided instead of being stalked, he would be the stalker. He made the statement, "What one man can do, another man can do." Together, they killed the bear.[8]

This statement has been proven over and over again in history. Feats and records were rated impossible. However, when they were achieved or broken by one person, a flock of others soon followed. When you see someone else do something, it helps you to believe you can do it, too.

A similarity occurs in Christianity. Many people say they do not need to go to church to be a Christian. Yet, normally without regular church attendance, most cannot maintain a healthy spiritual status. What would a church be if it had no meetings? It would not really be a church, would it? In this business, people need the meetings to renew and strengthen their faith in their company, their products, and themselves. Such gatherings will help you deal with and overcome the barrage of unbelief, doubt and rejection that is involved with leadership and building your own business.

THIRD STEP: Know your up-line and company distributor leaders, and see that your people do, too.

You should introduce yourself to all of your up-line leaders. If you have a nine-level compensation plan, then nine people above you are getting paid from your efforts. You should meet them and develop a relationship. Learn about their stories, past vocations, hobbies, families, and so on. Then, as you make contacts, you will know who in your up-line they may relate to the best. For example, I have a former air-conditioning repairman in my up-line. I like to introduce him to prospects from similar backgrounds such as construction, home service, and the like. I have others in my up-line who have professional backgrounds that I introduce to prospects and new distributors with like experience.

I want my distributors and prospects to meet as many people in my up-line as soon as possible. There is great persuasion in numbers. My grandson asked if he could have his sixteenth birthday party at my house. He said he would only have about seven or eight people. I said, "Sure." A couple of days later, he asked if he could have a couple more. I said, "Sure." By the time he had the party, there were twenty-four people there. As one person found out another person was going, that person wanted to go, too. People do not want to be left out—hence the phrase, "Everybody's doing it."

BOTTOM LINE:

Even the Lone Ranger had Tonto! Batman had Robin. If you think about it, every other superhero had a side kick! In reality, Jesus sent his disciples out in pairs. The point is this—we really do need others. We cannot do this business by ourselves. Don't even try!

~"You will be the same person five years from now, except for the books you read and the people you associate with."

– Charles "Tremendous" Jones~

Chapter 14

Octopus
Syndrome

Do you have the *Octopus* Syndrome? An octopus has eight arms reaching out in all directions. Are you often going in several different directions? Do you get easily side-tracked by other business opportunities? Do you tend to try to do more than one network marketing business at a time? You believe that two or more businesses complement one another, rather than competing with each other. The key issue to the *Octopus* Syndrome is *staying focused.*

Have you ever viewed *Animal Planet* on television and observed a cheetah hunting for lunch among a herd of deer? He picks out one deer and runs past other prey. He may even bump into potential meals, but he refuses to take his eyes off of that one deer he has chosen. He tracks it down and makes the kill.

Lion trainers often have a chair in one hand and a whip in the other. Have you ever wondered why they carry a chair? The undersized chair looks somewhat puny compared to the lion's massive jaws, razor-sharp teeth, and powerful claws. If the lion wanted to attack the trainer, the chair would offer little defense. The reason the trainer uses a chair is because it has four legs which causes the lion to lose focus, unable to stare at only one leg. The lion becomes distracted by the options, and the trainer uses this lack of focus to his advantage.

~"The eagle that chases two rabbits catches neither."
– Native American Proverb~

The Apostle Paul said, "Brethren, I do not count myself to have apprehended; but *one thing I do,* forgetting those things which are behind and reaching forward to those things which are ahead, I press toward the goal for the prize of the upward call of God in Christ Jesus" (Philippians 3:13-14, italics mine).

~Paul declared, "One thing I do," not, "Fifty things I dabble at."~

The Apostle James stated, "A double-minded man is unstable in all of his ways" (James 1:8 KJV). Other translations render it as follows: "Being a man of two minds, undecided in every step he takes" (Weymouth Translation); "Double-minded creature that he is, wavering at every turn" (Moffatt Translation); "He's half-hearted...wavering in everything he does" (Beck Translation).

3-STEP PLAN FOR STAYING FOCUSED

FIRST STEP: Watch out for distractions!

Maybe you have heard the expression, "All roads lead to Rome." That may be true, but if you took *every* road that leads to Rome, you would never reach Rome. You would just go around in circles. Some people pick a new network marketing business every six months. They are ready for the newest and hottest, but they never really go anywhere. They fritter away precious energy, jumping from one opportunity to another. At first, the other business venture may seem more attractive, but not everything is as it seems.

~Do you know why the grass is greener on the other side of the fence? It is because your neighbor's *septic tank* leaks.~

Beware of conversations that begin with any of the following statements: "I know the perfect networking company that'll complement what you are doing," "Since you are already using your phone, this phone card business would be a perfect fit," and, "If you sign up for my business, it'll be the perfect lead generator for you." And, of course, there is the one that goes, "This is a non-competing business, and it will complement your other company." That is a falsehood—*a lie!* Networking takes focus, and even if the products do not compete, building in one company competes with building in another company. You can use products from more than one networking company, but you cannot effectively build a business in two different companies at the same time.

The *Octopus* Syndrome is dangerous because it is very contagious and quickly spreads down-line. Your group will soon become unfocused, and their sponsoring efforts centered on each other. The dumbest thing you can do in networking is to get your people using another product from another networking company. You sell two things to your group—your products and the tools to sell your business and products. You do not sell other companies' products to your distributors. I have seen distributors get involved in lead businesses that are networking companies. They start off to buy leads to build their business. Pretty soon, they are trying to sell the lead business to other distributors instead of using the leads to build their own business. They will even have their own down-line doing the same, and then they will work on cross-line. This strategy is a catastrophe for business.

SECOND STEP: Remain committed.

Commit means "to bind or obligate as by pledge or assurance."[1] When you commit to something, it is like putting your car in gear. There is an internal force available to drive the car forward. When you get distracted, you are putting your business in neutral. If you get others distracted, you are putting their business in neutral, too.

Trust me on this one. You will never make as much money working two different companies as you do by focusing on one. You will have two unhealthy businesses until one or both die. Make enough money from one networking company so that you can invest in real estate, shopping centers, and the like. That is the way to diversify.

THIRD STEP: Believe in what you are doing.

Henry Ford said, "Whether you think you can or whether you think you can't, you're right." In Matthew 21:21, Jesus replied to his disciples, "Assuredly, I say to you, if you have faith and do not doubt, you will not only do what was done to the fig tree, but also if you say to this mountain, 'Be removed and be cast into the sea,' it will be done." In Mathew 17:20, he said that "if you have faith as a mustard seed...nothing will be impossible for you."

I am not saying you can "blab it and grab it." It takes courage, work, and focus to see yourself achieving. You must see yourself capable of achieving your goals. You must see it as a reality show and not as a cartoon. James 1:6-7 states, "But let him ask in faith, with no doubting, for he who doubts is like a wave of the sea driven and tossed by the wind. For let not that man suppose that he will receive anything from the Lord." If you want to achieve, you must believe.

Believe in what you are doing. When others speak negatively about networking, your company, or your product, it will challenge *your* belief. Ask yourself the following key question: "Are they going to persuade me, or will I persuade them?" Whoever feels most strongly will eventually win.

You have to believe that what you are doing is the very best use of your time and networking efforts. Make that decision and stick with it. Do not be seduced by other opportunities. Dance with the one that brought you!

BOTTOM LINE

Resolve to stay focused. Finish what you start. Do not start something new until you have reached the top of what you are doing. Be tremendously successful at one thing, rather than mediocre at a myriad of things.

Chapter 15

Foreign Missionary
Syndrome

Do you have the *Foreign Missionary* Syndrome? This condition is similar to a missionary willing to share the Gospel with total strangers on foreign soil in an unfamiliar culture, yet would never go next door to speak with a neighbor. If you have this syndrome, you refuse to share the business with your personal *center of influence.* You prefer a cold market of advertising to strangers, rather than sharing with family and friends in a warm market. The issues are *fear* and *conviction.*

It is normal to share with your friends whatever is happening in your life. You would tell them if you bought new clothes, a car, or even a television. If you bought an ice cream shop, you would invite all of your friends to come and try it out. It would be on the tip of your tongue when you saw them. You would keep asking them to come by until they did. After a while, if they did not check out your ice cream shop, you might stop asking them out of fear of running them off. Even so, you would believe it to be acceptable and customary to invite them. It should also be normal to invite them to find out about your network business.

Usually, the *Foreign Missionary* Syndrome reveals a lack of confidence in the product, the industry, or your own abilities. Maybe, you just do not trust your friends to treat your ideas with respect. If friends are going to criticize you for attempting to better yourself, perhaps you have the wrong friends (just a thought!).

Now I certainly believe in advertising. It is very likely that you have seen me on television or heard my ads on the radio. I think advertising is a great use of funds if you can afford it. But if you do not have enough conviction to share your business with those you already know, you do not have enough conviction to build a business on advertising alone.

3-STEP PLAN FOR OVERCOMING A LACK OF CONVICTION

FIRST STEP: Get the right perspective.

You are not in the business of persuading. You show the opportunity to others and let them make their own decision. Whether they decide to do it or not is out of your control. All you can do is share the story. Share the story with as many people as possible and let them decide whether it is right for them or not. Accept their decision.

SECOND STEP: Give those closest to you time and space.

"Jesus said…, 'A prophet is not without honor except in his own country and in his own house'" (Matthew 13:57). Do not expect all, or even the majority, of your personal contacts to be interested. That is okay. You do not need everyone you know to get involved; you just need a few. You find a few who find a few, and so forth. You do not need very many diamonds to have a fortune.

Do not give up on family and friends. Give them time. When they tell you, "No," they are not really saying, "No." They are saying, "Let's see what you do, first." They fully expect you to try this business for a few months and quit. They probably will not join you until they are convinced that you will go on without them. If you go on and build the business, some will come along within days, some within months, and some within years. However, some will never join you. The point is that you shared it with them and gave them the opportunity to choose for themselves.

THIRD STEP: Know your place.

Many times I have sat in a church service and when someone would ask me if the chair beside me was saved, I would tell them, "I don't think so. Let's pray for it and see if we can get it saved!" I guess my strange sense of humor thinks that is funny. A true missionary understands that they do not do the saving; they do the sharing. They share the faith, the message, or the story. Then, it is up to each one to make a decision about what to do with it. It is not your job to sell or persuade your friends, but only to share the story or deliver the message.

Network marketing is too simple of a concept to make hard. Either people see it or they don't. If everyone wanted to do it, they would not pay us who work hard and build a large business so much money. A few of your friends may want to join you, but many will not. That is okay; you do not need them all. Give them the right to make their own decisions. Do not take it personally. It is each one's decision—respect it.

~ *Foreign Missionary* Syndrome ~

The only way you can really do it wrong with your friends is to try and make the decision for them. You do that by deciding beforehand that they will not be interested and making the decision for them by not sharing it at all. You also do it by not respecting their decisions if they decide not to join you in the business.

~A very important reason to show the business to everyone you know is so that you do not attend a meeting sometime and find one of your friends or relatives there with someone else.~

BOTTOM LINE:

If you are not sold on your products and the network marketing business model, then you will not sell others. Sell yourself first. Then build your business!

Chapter 16

I've Arrived
Syndrome

Do you have the *I've Arrived* Syndrome? You have worked hard reaching many of your goals and have a fairly solid business. You feel that you may have earned the right to slack off…at least a little. You take a month off thinking your current level of performance will not be jeopardized. The key issue of the *I've Arrived* Syndrome is *loss of momentum*.

If you feel that you have arrived, then *you have!* And, you will *go no further*! Even the Apostle Paul said, "Not that I have already *attained*" (Philippians 3:12). In other words, Paul did not consider himself to have arrived or already won the battle. If you think you have arrived, you are about to lose momentum.

At any given time, you will have three distinct groups within your business: individuals leaving, others coming in, and those that are actually working. This fact is the same in all businesses. The goal is to keep enough momentum to have a greater number coming in and working than leaving.

It is said that a reporter was on an air flight with William Wrigley Jr., the founder of the Wrigley Gum empire, and he asked him why he continued to advertise so much. He was the leader in the business, and his company was flourishing. Wrigley answered, "It took a lot of thrust to get this plane in the air. We are now at cruising height. You wouldn't want the pilot to shut off the engines, would you?" Even an established business must maintain momentum, or it will eventually fall.

It takes a lot less effort to maintain a business than to build one. Nevertheless, you must keep enough effort going to keep it in the air. You will make more money for less effort in networking than anything else you could possibly do, but you will always need to keep up some effort. The more established leaders you have in your organization, the less time it will take to keep things going and growing. Even so, you should always know the state of your business and maintain a consistent level of momentum.

As a marketing professional, be careful to *watch your volume each month.* If you drop in sales three months in a row, then you are officially in a slump. If you are in a slump, you may ask, "What can I do to get out of a slump?" Good question! *When in a slump, work your way out!* Plan your comeback, and immediately set activity goals for yourself. You cannot control results, but you can control activity. Results will follow activity. You need to put on a full-court press to get things going again.

3-STEP PLAN FOR MAINTAINING MOMENTUM

FIRST STEP: Retain relationships within your organization.

Do not neglect your group. Find effective ways to communicate with them. Use voice mail, conference calls, and event meetings to support them. Spend time with your people.

There is no retention without relationships, and no relationship without occasional *face-to-face and phone* contact. Emails must be followed up with personal contact. You cannot convey passion and importance through email.

There are three levels of relationships. The objective is to move everyone to the next level. The *first level* consists of people that *know you.* You have met these individuals and have shared a conversation; however, there is little depth of relationship. These relationships are not established enough to maintain ongoing business.

The *second level* consists of people that *like you.* As it is often said, "Nobody cares how much you know until they know how much you care."[1] This business differs from other businesses—it is a voluntary army. People can defect at any time. If they like you, they will be prone to stay. If they do not like you, they will soon be gone.

The *third level* consists of people that *trust you.* If you do not bond, you will not build. If a bond is broken, you will lose business. Trust is essential for this deepest level.

~Trust is the currency of teamwork.~

Trust is like money—the more you have, the more your options increase. If you do not have any money, then your choices are few. If you have built trust, then you will be able to accomplish great things. George Barna in *The Power of Team Leadership* stated, "One of the keys to successful teamwork is the nature and depth of the relationships developed among team members. Examining the level of community among the members of a team is a telltale sign of their maturity and potential."[2] You can build trust by simply following these principles:

- Be a *good*-finder, and not a fault-finder.
- Find someone to encourage every day.
- Keep your promises.
- Do not exaggerate.
- Make everything better.
- Lead by example.

~ *I've Arrived* Syndrome ~

SECOND STEP: Retain a relationship with the products for yourself and your group.

When I first bought a lake house, I admired the beautiful view and thought of how lucky I was to have it. After a while, I started taking that view for granted. I noticed that, many times, I would not even take the time to look at it.

People eventually take the products for granted. They use them every day, and after a while, they forget how good the products made them feel in the beginning. When people begin using health products, they are used to feeling lousy, but then they feel great. However, after a while on the products, they get used to feeling good. For some reason, they stop relating their current feelings to the products. Some people then stop using them. For a time, they do not notice any difference. However, if they go back to their old habits, in days, weeks, or years they will be right back where they were —sometimes worse—before they first started using the products. The products are working just as well as they did in the beginning, but people take their new level of health (product satisfaction) for granted. They do not remember how it was before using the product. When they return to using the product, it may take days, weeks, or months to get back to that same level as when they first began using it. Journaling the benefits received in the very beginning is the most reliable way to measure product benefits over a long period of time.

Therefore, be sure to take regular time during events and calls for product testimonials. Have people share the benefits they enjoy from the products. Testimonials do not need to be long; from one to three minutes, in most cases, is enough. Having several different people share about different products will get more people involved and allow a greater number of listeners to relate.

It is imperative that you become a product of your products. In other words, build your own life story and testimonials around your use of the products. Pardon my sarcasm, but the best thing you can do when you first get started is to gather up all of the other products you were using before you began your networking business, put them in a bag in the closet, and replace them with the products from your company. Then after three to six months, when you have thoroughly learned all of the benefits of your products and how best to use them, you can take the bag of previously used products and give them away to someone you don't care about.

THIRD STEP: Retain a relationship with your company.

Read everything you can about your company. Be aware of new products and policies. Know what is on the company's website. If you are not on the company email list, *get on it!* With today's email and spam protectors, it is possible that even if you were once getting company emails, you may no longer be receiving them. It is your responsibility to correct this issue. It is your business; you must know what the company is doing in a timely manner. So contact customer service to be sure you are getting company emails. Also, remind your distributors to do the same.

Attend your company conventions and sponsored events. In addition, I recommend traveling to the company headquarters sometime and seeing it in person. This experience makes your business more tangible and real. It is also a great way to gain confidence in your company.

BOTTOM LINE:

Remember that your networking business is an army of volunteers. At any given time, you will have those coming in, some leaving, and others working. Everything is about *choice*. To retain relationships, strive to be *likeable* and always build *trust*.

Conclusion

I am totally convinced that the leveraging factor of networking can give you the ability to earn from two to five times more per hour of work. Networking will give you the opportunity to achieve beyond your wildest dreams. Your level of achievement is entirely up to you. You can earn just a few hundred dollars per month for some extra income, or you can earn millions. It is your choice. This industry is not on trial; it has already proven itself. Grab it, embrace it, and enjoy it. It will give you a level of freedom and success that is rarely obtainable in business or a job. Don't question it—just do it.

Oh, and by the way…How in the world are you, anyway?

To contact Andy Willoughby, email him at
Andy@3stepplan.com.

Acknowledgments

*I*t is important to recognize all of those who have helped bring this book to the public. First, I want to thank my wife, Brenda. With over forty years together, the knowledge that was accumulated in this book was mostly learned and experienced jointly. Many times, her continued support and faithfulness were the only perseverance I had. Brenda is much more than a cheerleader; she is a teammate that has offered an equal contribution to any success I have achieved.

I want to echo that remark for my dear friend and co-author, Dr. David Baldwin, concerning his wife, Sandy. David often shared with me how his marriage with Sandy had enriched his life. They were a joyful and powerful couple that inspired thousands on multiple continents. It should also be mentioned that, due to David's untimely death, Sandy valiantly picked up David's load to finish this book. At a time when she was most weakened, she showed great strength.

~ Acknowledgments ~

Also, our editor, Michelle Zipfel, worked many hours with a loving heart over every word in this book. As David's daughter-in-law, her efforts have truly honored his memory. Finally, our graphic artist, Ryan Skjervem, patiently dealt with every change and alteration with skill and grace.

In conclusion, since family has been the priority in both David's and my life, it is fitting to acknowledge our children and grandchildren, who have enriched our lives and continually given us purpose in our careers.

Notes

Preface
1. John Godzich, *First Things First* (Lehi, UT: XGoPro, LLC), 25.
2. *Webster's Universal College Dictionary* (New York, NY: Gramercy Books, 1997), 799.

Introduction
1. John Godzich, *First Things First*, 27.
2. Sabrina Tavernise, "Boeing's Russian Edge," *New York Times*, May 26, 2001, Business Day section.
3. Presented by Anthony J. Interlandi, "Small Business Development Trust," Embassy of the United States: Georgetown-Guyana, Posted on June 29, 2005.
http://georgetown.usembassy.gov/guyana/small_business_interlandi_speech.html

Chapter 1: *Impossible Dream* Syndrome
1. Woodrow Kroll, *God's Guide for Life's Choices: Drawing Wisdom from the Book of Proverbs* (Ann Arbor, MI: Servant Publications, 2003), 101.
2. Bo Bennett, *Year to Success* (Sudbury, MA: Archieboy Holdings, L.L.C., 2006), 8.
3. Dr. Richard D. Dobbins, *Emotional Power* (Old Tappan, NJ: Fleming H. Revell Co., 1984), 41.
4. Brian Tracy, *The 100 Absolutely Unbreakable Laws of Business Success* (San Francisco: Berrett-Koehler Publishers, Inc., 2000), 17.
5. John Hammond (ed.), *The Fine Art of Doing Better* (Scottsdale, AZ: American Motivational Assoc., 1974), 114.

~ Notes ~

6. E. Glenn Wagner with Steve Halliday, *Escape From Church Inc.: The Return of the Pastor-Shepherd* (Grand Rapids, MI: Zondervan, 1999), 76.
7. *Webster's Universal College Dictionary*, 178.

Chapter 2: *Bogeyman* Syndrome
1. Charles E. Barnhart, Jr., "Choose Wisely!" From the Desk of Deacon Charlie, Keysville Evangelical Lutheran Church.
   http://www.emmitsburg.net/klc/deacon_charlie/2005/choose_wisely.htm
2. Brian Tracy, *The 100 Absolutely Unbreakable Laws of Business Success*, 124.
3. Ron Baker, "Earning My Mouse Ears, Part III: The Disney Approach to Customer Loyalty," Community Section, VeraSage Institute.
   http://www.verasage.com/index.php/community/2007/05/

Chapter 3: *Cheese and Whine* Syndrome
1. Peggy Anderson, *Great Quotes From Great Leaders* (Lombard, IL: Great Quotations, Inc., 1989), 71.

Chapter 4: *Mañana* Syndrome
1. *Webster's Universal College Dictionary*, 630.
2. Walt Kallestad & Steve Schey, *Total Quality Ministry* (Minneapolis: Augsburg, 1994), 61.
3. Napoleon Hill, Think & Grow Rich (New York, NY: Fawcett Crest Book, 1960), 139.
4. Anthony Robbins, *Awaken the Giant Within: How to Take Immediate Control of Your Mental, Emotional, Physical and Financial Destiny!* (New York, NY: Summit Books, 1991), 39.
5. Leonard Sweet, Brian D. McLaren, Jerry Hasselmayer, A *Is For Abductive: The Language of the Emerging Church* (Grand Rapid, MI: Zondervan, 2003), 110.
6. Dr. Laurence J. Peter, *Peter's Quotations: Ideas for Our Time* (New York, NY: William Morrow and Co., Inc., 1977), 100.
7. Dr. Laurence J. Peter, *Peter's Quotations: Ideas for Our Time*, 100.
8. Joe Calhoon and Bruce Jeffrey, *Prioritize! A System for Leading Your Business and Life on Purpose* (Sevierville, TN: Insight Publishing, 2005), 131.

Chapter 5: *Einstein* Syndrome
1. "Motivational Zig Ziglar Quotes," Great Inspirational Quotes to Inspire Life Moments.
   http://www.great-inspirational-quotes.com/zig-ziglar-quotes.html

~ Notes ~

2. John Maxwell, *The Success Journey: The Process of Living Your Dreams* (Nashville, TN: Thomas Nelson, 1997), 106.

Chapter 6: Pass the Buck Syndrome
1. W. Steven Brown, *13 Fatal Errors Managers Make and How You Can Avoid Them* (New York, NY: Berkley Books, 1985), 2.
2. William H. Johnson (1901-1970), 20th century American artist.
3. Max E. Anders, *30 Days to Understanding the Christian Life* (Brentwood, TN: Wolgemuth and Hyatt Publishers, Inc., 1990), 43.

Chapter 9: *Missing Link* Syndrome
1. Brian Banashak, *The Little Book of Business Wisdom: Practical Insights for Entrepreneurs, Professionals and Business Owners* (Mobile, AL: Evergreen Press, 2000), 1.

Chapter 10: *Hobby* Syndrome
1. Joe Calhoon and Bruce Jeffrey, *Prioritize! A System for Leading Your Business and Life On Purpose*, 76.
2. Dr. Ronald Cottle, *Lectures On Leadership: Volume I* (Columbus, GA: TEC Publications, 2004), 8.
3. Brian Tracy, *The 100 Absolutely Unbreakable Laws of Business Success*, 294.
4. Lucy Mead, *Graduates Are Special* (New York: Gramercy Books, 2001), 50.
5. Alan Loy McGinnis, *The Balanced Life: Achieving Success in Work and Love* (Minneapolis: Augsburg, 1997), 84.

Chapter 12: *Jack-in-the-Box* Syndrome
1. John Mason, *The Impossible is Possible* (Minneapolis: Bethany House, 2003), 117.

Chapter 13: *Lone Ranger* Syndrome
1. David Ferguson, *The Great Commandment Principle* (Wheaton, IL: Tyndale House, 1998), 27.
2. Steve Brown, *Follow the Wind: Our Lord, The Holy Spirit* (Grand Rapids, MI: Baker Books, 1999), 131.
3. Alan Loy McGinnis, *The Balanced Life: Achieving Success In Work and Love* (Minneapolis: Augsburg, 1997), 10.
4. *Webster's Universal College Dictionary*, 799.
5. Laurie Beth Jones, *Teach Your Team to Fish: Using Ancient Wisdom for Inspired Teamwork* (New York, NY: Crown Business, 2002), xi.

~ Notes ~

6. John C. Maxwell, *The 17 Indisputable Laws of Teamwork* (Nashville: Thomas Nelson Publishers, 2001), 23.
7. Stan Toler & Larry Gilbert, *The Pastor's Playbook: Coaching Your Team for Ministry* (Kansas City, MO: Beacon Hill Press of Kansas City, 2000), 9.
8. *The Edge,* directed by Lee Tamahori, Twentieth Century Fox, 1997.

Chapter 14: *Octopus* Syndrome
1. *Webster's Universal College Dictionary*, 162.
2. Bo Bennett, *Year to Success*, 8.

Chapter 16: *I've Arrived* Syndrome
1. Cassis-Michel Reggon and Bob Phillips, *The All-American Quote Book* (Eugene, OR: Harvest House Publishers, 1995), 50.
2. George Barna, *The Power of Team Leadership: Finding Strength in Shared Responsibility* (Colorado Springs, CO: Water Brook Press, 2001), 168.